Carry a Big Stick

THE UNCOMMON HEROISM OF THEODORE ROOSEVELT

GEORGE GRANT

LEADERS IN ACTION SERIES

Highland Books

Carry a Big Stick:
The Uncommon Heroism of Theodore Roosevelt

ISBN 0-9645396-6-7
Copyright © 1996 by George Grant

Published by Highland Books
229 South Bridge Street
P.O. Box 254
Elkton, MD 21922-0254
Tel. (410) 392-5554
Send requests for information to the above address.

Printed in the United States of America.

TABLE OF CONTENTS

ACKNOWLEDGMENTS

*If I preach to you anything which I do not strive,
with whatever haltings and shortcomings, myself to
realize, then I am unworthy your paying heed to me.*[1]

*"B*iographical labors are inevitably the fruit of childhood ideals," stated Scottish historian John
Buchan. "The seeds sown in early years bear a harvest of
intellectual wonderment in latter years."[2]

Indeed, my father first introduced me to the life and
exploits of Theodore Roosevelt. When I was a young boy he
gave me a small chapbook that became one of my most
prized possessions. It still is. Later, he encouraged my fasci-
nation with this great man by taking me to sites associated
with his varied career. The seeds my father sowed so many
years ago continue to bear much fruit in my life–and for that
I will always be grateful.

The good people at both Highland Books and
Cumberland House also heartily encouraged me in pursuing
my interests in Roosevelt. Phil Hibbard, Will Wallace, Heather
Armstrong, Ron Pitkin, and Dean Andreola have been far
more patient and generous than I could have ever asked.

In addition, a number of other friends and fellow-labor-
ers have urged me to press ahead with this book and the
leadership series of which it is a part–and, at the same time
have helped to support the work of the King's Meadow Study

Center so that I could. I can't imagine doing without the gracious encouragement of David Drye, Joe Costello, Paige Overton, Scott Roley, Jackie Lusk, or Randy Terry. Jerry and Cindy Walton, Bill and Robin Amos, Tom and Sylvia Singleton, Tom and Jody Clark, Bill and Sharon Taylor, Jim and Gwen Smith, Bill and Dawn Ruff, Darrow and Marilyn Miller, Jeff and Karla Kessler, Ron and Jean Nash, Rich and Liz Mays, Steve and Marijean Green, and Steve and Annie Chapman all have been selfless supporters from the beginning. Dale and Ann Smith, Stephen and Trish Mansfield, Steve and Wendy Wilkins, Gene and Susan Hunt, Tom and Yo Clark, and David and Diane Vaughan guided me through many a rocky shoal with their wise counsel and friendship.

Mike Hyatt first suggested that I consider turning my writing proclivities toward biographies. Jan Dennis, David Dunham, and Robert Wolgemuth gave me my first opportunities to try my hand at this rather demanding discipline. And Otto Scott pointed the way for me by providing the appropriate models from which to learn.

The soundtrack for this project was provided by Michael Card, Anuna, Deanta, and Anthony Hopkins; the midnight musings were provided by Richard Weaver, Colin Thubron, Hilaire Belloc, and G.K. Chesterton.

To all these, I offer my sincerest thanks.

I suppose I probably ought to mention the Nine Muses, the Three Graces, and the Merry Band of Joyeuse Garde as well; but the fact is my greatest and best inspiration comes from my family. Karen is without a doubt a "help meet" for me. And Joel, Joanna, and Jesse are the pride of my life. Their love and unwavering faithfulness remain my greatest hope and richest resource. To them I owe my all in all.

King's Meadow Farm
Pentecost 1996

INTRODUCTION

Every great nation owes to the men whose lives
have formed part of its greatness not merely the
material effect of what they did, not merely the laws
they placed upon the statute books or the victories
they won over armed foes, but also the immense but
indefinable moral influence produced by their deeds
and words themselves upon the national character.[3]

*B*y any measure Theodore Roosevelt was a remarkable man. Before his fiftieth birthday he had served
as a New York state legislator, the under-secretary of the Navy,
police commissioner for the city of New York, U.S. civil service
commissioner, the governor of the state of New York, the vice-
president under William McKinley, a colonel in the U.S. Army,
and two terms as the president of the United States.

In addition, he had run a cattle ranch in the Dakota
Territories, served as a reporter and editor for several journals, newspapers, and magazines, and conducted scientific
expeditions on four continents. He read at least five books
every week of his life and wrote nearly fifty on an astonish-
ing array of subjects–from history and biography to natural
science and social criticism.

He enjoyed hunting, boxing, and wrestling. He was an
amateur taxidermist, botanist, ornithologist, and astronomer.
He was a devoted family man who lovingly raised six children.
And he enjoyed a life-long romance with his wife.

During his long and varied career, he was hailed by supporters and rivals alike as the greatest man of the age–perhaps one of the greatest of all ages.[4] According to Thomas Reed, Speaker of the House of Representatives, he was a "new-world Bismark and Cromwell combined."[5] President Grover Cleveland described him as "one of the ablest men yet produced in human history."[6] Senator Henry Cabot Lodge asserted that, "Since Caesar, perhaps no one has attained among crowded duties and great responsibilities, such high proficiency in so many separate fields of activity."[7] After an evening in his company, the epic poet Rudyard Kipling wrote, "I curled up on the seat opposite and listened and wondered until the universe seemed to be spinning round–and Roosevelt was the spinner."[8] Great Britain's Lord Charnwood exclaimed, "No statesman for centuries has had his width of intellectual range; to be sure no intellectual has so touched the world with action."[9] Even his life-long political opponent, William Jennings Bryan, was bedazzled by his prowess. "Search the annals of history if you will," he said. "Never will you find a man more remarkable in every way than he."[10]

The times that this remarkable man lived in were themselves quite remarkable–the sunset of one century and the dawning of another. The United States had grown from sixteen states in 1800 to forty-five in 1900, from nine hundred thousand square miles to almost four million, and from a population of five million to seventy-six million. That century had produced steamships, railroads, streetcars, bicycles, roller-skates, the air brake, the torpedo, telephones, telegraphs, transatlantic cables, harvesting machines, threshers, cotton gins, cooking ranges, sewing machines, phonographs, type-writers, electric lights, illuminating gas, photographs, x-rays, motion pictures, and cottonseed oil. According to journalist

Edward Byrn, the comparison of the start of the century with the end of the century was "like the juxtaposition of a distant star with the noonday sun."[11] And, popular historian M.J. de Forest Shelton exclaimed that there was "more difference between Napoleon's day and ours than between Napoleon's and Julius Caesar's. One century against eighteen."[12] English intellectual Frederic Harrison agreed:

> *Take it all in all, the merely material, physical, mechanical change in human life in the hundred years, from the days of Watt and Arkwright to our own, is greater than occurred in the thousand years that preceded, perhaps even the two thousand or twenty thousand years.*[13]

Despite bitter labor agitation, anarchist strikes, communist insurgencies, and the emergence of terrorism as a political weapon; despite attempts on the lives of the Prince of Wales, the German Emperor, and the Shah of Persia; despite successful assassinations of King Umberto of Italy and President McKinley; despite the uproar of the Dreyfus affair in France and the Robida scandal in Austria; despite the imminent passing of the old world order with its accompanying specter; despite everything, a robust optimism pervaded the thinking of most Westerners. Their advances, after all, had been stunning. So, for the most part, they shared the opinion of the *New York World* in its prediction that the new century would "meet and overcome all perils and prove to be the best that this steadily improving planet has ever seen."[14]

Theodore Roosevelt had a saner view–a more realistic view–of his time. It was a view balanced by a Christian understanding of mankind–made in the very image of God, but at the same time, fallen. Perhaps that is the most remarkable thing about this remarkable man: he actually understood his remarkable times and what remarkable things had to be done in order to sustain them.

Roosevelt saw all too clearly the dark dangers that loomed as the Western world marched so boldly, so confidently, into the twentieth century. That is why he devoted himself to remedying as many dangers as possible throughout his life. His political crusades and social reforms focused on the poor working man, on the struggling immigrant, on the miserable tenement dweller, on the helpless widow and orphan, on the despised victims of racial or ethnic prejudice, and on the pioneering homesteader.

By the taint of today's rigidly ideological standards, he was a bundle of contradictions and cross-purposes: sometimes he coursed to the left, sometimes to the right; sometimes he was a champion of mugwumps and progressives, sometimes of standpats and monopolists; sometimes he was the guardian of labor, sometimes of capital; sometimes he was the voice of hawkish expansionism, sometimes of dovish nationalism. But to Roosevelt, there was never a contradiction in his seemingly conflicting positions. In fact, he was unswayed–and even repelled–by the traditional categories of partisanism. Instead, he tenaciously pursued the path of truth and justice–wherever. To this day he is a sort of universal hero: captive to no single interest, no single party, and no single movement. It was almost as if he were above the petty fray.

Perhaps then, the reason he continues to stand out as one of the greatest leaders in the history of the United States is this: he was willing to use his dynamic accomplishments and prescient gifts for the good of all those around him and of all those who would come after him–regardless of the possible political or career consequences. That kind of moral and intellectual heroism is highly uncommon in this day of standardless pragmatism and cunning latitudinarianism.

This book, the second in a series of biographical profiles of leaders in action, is designed to give modern readers a glimpse of the character that made possible Theodore Roosevelt's uncommon independence of heart, mind, and spirit–indeed, his uncommon heroism. It is certainly not intended to be a comprehensive look at his life and work–there are many fine biographies that succeed at that task–rather, it focuses on the lessons that his character, moral fiber, and faith have to offer us in this woefully over-managed but under-led culture.

The first section affords a quick overview of the great man's life. It traces his triumphs and tragedies with an eye toward understanding how he was able to weave a fabric of life-long success in accord with the glad tidings of providence.

The second section focuses on thirty essential character traits that typified Roosevelt's career, relationships, and habits of life. What were the disciplines of mind and morals, what were the priorities of heart and soul, what were the passions of spirit and flesh that drove him to such heights as he attained?

Finally, in the third section, the lessons of Roosevelt's great legacy are examined in light of the needs of our own time. How can we learn from him to answer the challenges of today?

Generally, we moderns hold to a strangely disjunctive view of the relationship between life and work–thus enabling us to nonchalantly separate a person's private character from his public accomplishments. But this novel divorce of root from fruit, however genteel, is a ribald denial of one of the most basic truths in life: what you are begets what you do. Wrong-headed philosophies stem from wrong-headed philosophers; yet orthodoxy invariably begets orthopraxy. Sin does not just happen; it is sinners that sin. Likewise, heroes do not simply emerge ex nihilo; heroes are forged upon the anvil of ethical faithfulness.

English historian and journalist Hilaire Belloc noted, "Biography always affords the greatest insights into sociology. To comprehend the history of a thing is to unlock the mysteries of its present, and more, to discover the profundities of its future."[15] Similarly, the inimitable Samuel Johnson quipped, "Almost all the miseries of life, almost all the wickedness that infects society, and almost all the distresses that afflict mankind, are the consequences of some defect in private duties. Likewise, all the joys of this world may be attributable to the happiness of hearth and home."[16]

Or, as E. Michael Jones has asserted, "Biography is destiny."[17]

It is my prayer that the example of Theodore Roosevelt portrayed within these pages will inspire a whole new generation of emerging leaders to attain to their destiny.

CHRONOLOGY OF THEODORE ROOSEVELT'S LIFE

We are better for the lives and deeds of our mighty men who have served the nation well[18]

1858   Theodore Roosevelt is born in New York City on October 27.

1865   With his brother and a childhood friend Edith Carrow, Theodore watches the funeral cortege of Abraham Lincoln from his parlor window.

1868   His parents take the entire family on a grand tour of Europe.

1875   His homeschooling experience concludes with a year of special tutoring in Latin, Greek, and mathematics–disciplines that figured prominently in the college entrance examinations of the day.

1876   He is accepted at Harvard College and takes rooms nearby in Cambridge.

1880   He graduates from Harvard University on June 30.

1880   He marries his Harvard sweetheart, Alice Lee, on October 27.

1881   He briefly studies law at New York University before deciding to enter public service.

1882   He is sworn in as the youngest New York state legislator.

1882   On a hill overlooking Oyster Bay on Long Island he builds a house–resplendent with porches and porticoes and brimming with his disposition and personality–later to be named Sagamore Hill.

1882   Written for the most part while in college, his first book, *The Naval War of 1812*, is published.

1883   After leading a successful legislative campaign to reform judicial and civil service appointments, he is re-elected by the widest margin of any legislator in New York.

1884	On February 14, both his wife and his mother tragically die–his wife while giving birth to his first child, Alice.
1884	In grief, he heads west to work on his cattle ranch in the Dakota Territories.
1886	He returns home and conducts an unsuccessful campaign for mayor of New York.
1886	He marries Edith Carrow on December 2.
1887	His biography of Thomas Hart Benton is published.
1887	On September 13, his first son, Ted Jr., is born.
1888	His long-awaited biography of Gouverneur Morris is published.
1889	He is appointed as a United States civil service commissioner and moves to Washington.
1889	The first volume of his renowned history, *The Winning of the West*, is published.
1889	On October 10, his second son, Kermit, is born.
1891	His history of New York City is published to rave reviews.
1891	On August 13, his second daughter, Ethel, is born.
1894	On April 10, his third son, Archie, is born.
1894	On August 14, after a long history of drinking, his brother Elliot dies in a tragic fall.
1895	He resigns his post in Washington to become president of the New York Police Board.
1895	He co-authors *Hero Tales from American History* with Henry Cabot Lodge.
1897	He is appointed assistant secretary of the Navy by President McKinley.
1897	On November 19, his fourth son, Quentin, is born.
1898	Commissioned an Army colonel, he raises a volunteer cavalry (the famed Rough Riders) to fight in the Spanish-American War.
1898	He returns from the war as a hero and is overwhelmingly elected Governor of New York on November 8.
1900	He is unanimously chosen to join incumbent William McKinley on the Republican ticket and is elected vice president on November 4.
1900	His best-selling book, *The Strenuous Life*, is published.

1901	President McKinley is shot on September 6 by an assassin while attending the Pan American Exposition in Buffalo.
1901	After appearing to make a quick recovery, the President succumbs from his wounds and Roosevelt is sworn in as his successor in September 14.
1901	His biography of Oliver Cromwell is published.
1902	His carefully researched scientific treatise, *The Deer Family*, is published.
1902	He successfully negotiates a settlement to a national coal strike.
1903	He dramatically enforces the Monroe Doctrine against European encroachment in Venezuela–winning for himself hero status throughout Latin America.
1903	He recognizes the secession of Panama from Columbia and initiates construction of the Panama Canal.
1904	On November 8, he is re-elected by the widest popular margin ever recorded by a presidential candidate on November 8.
1905	He secures the first workmen's compensation and employer's liability laws.
1906	On February 17, his daughter Alice marries Congressman Nicholas Longworth in a magnificent White House ceremony.
1906	After masterminding the peace treaty ending the Russian-Japanese War, he is awarded the Nobel Peace Prize.
1906	He outlines the solution of the Algeciras Conference, bringing peace to indigenous North Africans and the European colonial powers.
1907	He establishes the Roosevelt Foundation for Industrial Peace.
1907	He launches an historic around-the-world naval flotilla–the first circumnavigation of the globe by a national naval force.
1909	He retires to private life upon the expiration of his presidential term.
1909	On March 23, he sets sail for an African safari and a grand tour of Europe.
1910	He serves as Special Ambassador to England at the funeral of King Edward VII.
1910	He returns from abroad only to discover that his successor in the White House, William Taft, has compromised many of his most important policies and reforms.

1911	He becomes an editor for *Outlook* magazine.
1912	The publication of his book *Conservation of Womanhood and Childhood* launches a national movement resulting in new child and family labor laws.
1912	On February 25, he announces his candidacy for the presidency.
1912	Though he had won all but one primary and caucus, his delegates are barred from the Republican National Convention by the party establishment and the lackluster incumbent is re-nominated.
1912	Breaking with the Republican Party, he is nominated by the fledgling Progressive Party on August 7 and begins a vigorous campaign.
1912	Leading slightly in the polls, he is wounded in an assassination attempt on October 14 and is forced to sit out the vital final three weeks of the race.
1912	He easily outdistances Taft; however, the Democratic rival Woodrow Wilson is able to eke out a win on election day, November 5, with 41 percent of the vote.
1913	He embarks on a daring hunting and exploring adventure in the Brazilian Amazon where he is seriously injured, and contracts malaria–complications from which he will suffer for the rest of his life.
1916	His prophetic book, *Fear God and Take Your Own Part*, is published.
1917	He requests sanction to raise a volunteer battalion to fight in the First World War, but is denied permission by Wilson.
1918	All four of his sons are deployed on the German front.
1918	In February, Archie is seriously wounded.
1918	In July, Quentin is shot down behind enemy lines and dies–although immensely proud, he never fully recovers from the grief.
1919	He dies at Sagamore Hill on January 6.
1925	Congress approves Gutzon Borglum's plan for a massive sculpted memorial at Mount Rushmore to America's greatest statesmen–George Washington, Thomas Jefferson, Abraham Lincoln, and of course, Theodore Roosevelt.

Who goes there? An American!
Brain and spirit and brawn and heart,
'Twas for him that the nations spared
Each to the years its noblest part;
Till from the Dutch, the Gaul, the Celt
Blossomed the soul of Roosevelt.

Student, trooper, and gentleman
Level-lidded with times and kings,
His the voice for a comrade's cheer
His the ear when the saber rings.
Hero shades of the old days melt
In the quick pulse of Roosevelt.

Hand that's molded to hilt of sword;
Heart that ever has laughed at fear;
Type and pattern of civic pride;
Wit and grace of the cavalier;
All that his fathers prayed and felt
Gleams in the glance of Roosevelt.

Who goes there? An American!
Man to the core–as men should be.
Let him pass through the lines alone,
Type of the Sons of Liberty.
Here, where his fathers' fathers dwelt,
Honor and faith for Roosevelt.[19]

Grace Duffie Boylan

Part I:
The Life of Theodore Roosevelt

"Speak softly and carry a big stick; you will go far. It sounds rather as if that were but a homely old adage, yet as is often the case with matters of tradition, this truism is actually true."[20]

A BULL MOOSE

I feel as fit as a Bull Moose.[21]

*A*t a campaign stop in Milwaukee on the evening of October 14, 1912, a deranged, out-of-work bartender emerged from a crowd and shot Theodore Roosevelt in the chest at point-blank range. Staggered by the impact of the bullet and the shock of the injury, the great man nevertheless righted himself.

As the crowd converged on the man, the wounded former president cried, "Stand back! Don't hurt the man! Bring him to me!" After examining his would-be assassin with a dismissive glare, he told his aides to get him to the rally. "This may be the last speech I deliver," he admitted. Seeing that he was bleeding heavily, several doctors in Roosevelt's party wanted to rush him to the hospital at once, but he waved them aside. "You just stay where you are," he ordered. "I am going to make this speech and you might as well compose yourselves." When they persisted, he said, "Get an ambulance or a carriage or anything you like at ten o'clock and I'll go to the hospital, but I won't go until I've finished my speech." He then demanded that his driver proceed to the auditorium and said fervently, "I will make this speech or die. It is one thing or the other." [22]

When he reached the rally, the emcee announced that an attempt had been made on Roosevelt's life. But as he appeared on the platform, the familiar figure smiled and waved weakly to the awestruck crowd. "It is true," he whispered in a hoarse voice, "I have just been shot. But it takes more than that to kill a Bull Moose." [23]

Now beginning to gain his composure, he said, "Friends, I should ask you to be as quiet as possible. And please excuse me from making a long speech. I'll do the best I can." He then took his manuscript from his jacket; it had been pierced through by the bullet and was soaked with blood. "It is nothing," he said as the people gasped. "I am not hurt badly. I have a message to deliver and will deliver it as long as there is life in my body." The audience became deathly still as he went on to say, "I have had an A-1 time in life and I am having it now." [24]

He always had the ability to cast an intoxicating spell over crowds. Even now, his physical presence was dominating. His charisma was infectious. His passionate commitment to what he believed was right and good and true was dynamically compelling—even to those who opposed him politically.

Though by then he was bleeding profusely, he spoke for an hour and a half—waving off repeated appeals for him to stop and seek medical treatment. By the end he had almost completely regained his typical stump fervor—rousing the crowd to several extended ovations. When at last he allowed his concerned party to take him to the hospital, the audience reached a near frenzy chanting "Teddy! Teddy! Teddy!"

At the hospital he joked and talked politics with his attendants. But his condition was hardly a joking matter. The surgeons found that the bullet had fractured his fourth rib and lodged close to his right lung. "It is largely due to the fact that he is a physical marvel that he was not mortally wounded," observed one of them later. "He is one of the most powerful men I have ever seen on an operating table. The bullet lodged in the massive muscles of the chest instead of penetrating the lung." [25]

Nevertheless, he was no longer a young buck at 54. He was required–against his quite considerable will–to sit out the remainder of the campaign. Still, he lived to fight another day.

Later, his biographers would view the incident as quintessential Roosevelt: imposing the sheer force of his will upon a seemingly impossible circumstance, and yet prevailing. [26] From beginning to end, that was the story of his life. He was forever defying the odds, defying all reason, defying the very physical realities of life in this poor fallen world.

A SLOW START

I was a sickly, delicate boy, suffered much from asthma, and frequently had to be taken away on trips to find a place where I could breathe.[27]

Theodore Roosevelt, Junior, was born on October 27, 1858, in New York City. His father, Theodore Roosevelt, Senior, was a sixth generation New York burgher–the scion of one of the richest and most influential old Dutch families of Manhattan. By all accounts he displayed an exuberant, disciplined, and masculine joy of life. The child's mother, Martha Bulloch Roosevelt, was an unmistakable southern belle–the beautiful and delicate daughter of one of the most prominent Scottish plantation families of Georgia.

This child was the heir of two proud traditions which he would cherish for the rest of his life: the sturdy Dutch industrial mercantilism of the North and the romantic Scottish pioneer agrarianism of the South. Nicknamed Teedie, he grew up in a harmonious home where Yankee vigor and ingenuity was balanced by Dixie refinement and sophistication, masculine discipline by feminine gentleness, intellectual seriousness by intellectual inquisitiveness, the rewards of privilege by the responsibilities of charity, and the bustle of urbanity by the decorum of gentility. Into this happy home were shortly added two more siblings–a sister and a brother–so there was no lack of activity or companionship.

Two things, however, contrived to disturb Teedie's early idyllic existence. The first came five months after his second birthday. Despite repeated promises to withdraw threatening troop placements, President Abraham Lincoln suddenly ordered a massive reinforcement of the federal garrison at Fort Sumpter–situated in the strategic harbor of Charleston, South Carolina. As a result, hostilities erupted between North and South. The bitter war not only divided the land, it divided the Roosevelt household. Teedie's mother–as well as his Bulloch grandmother and aunt, who had come to live with the young family in New York–were unrepentant Confederate sympathizers. They participated in clandestine relief efforts–sending contraband supplies across the blockade lines–and kept in full communication with other Bulloch family members who were actively involved in the makeshift rebel military operations aimed at repulsing any and all Northern invaders. Indeed, they gaily hung the Stars and Bars from eaves of their midtown brownstone following the many Southern victories at the beginning of the conflict.

Teedie's father on the other hand was a passionate Unionist and a loyal Lincoln Republican. Though he could not in good conscience take up arms against his beloved Confederate in-laws, he was actively engaged in the federal war effort–working on behalf of the enlisted men on the front lines. For many months he lobbied in Washington, D.C., to secure legislation designed to provide financial stability and security for families the soldiers had left at home. Afterwards, he tirelessly sloughed through the mud of the freezing camps urging paymaster reforms and bolstering Yankee morale.

The long absences from the family that these activities required were especially felt by his young son. From the moment of his father's departure, Teedie's health began a precipitous decline. This was the second trial that contrived to disrupt his bucolic childhood. He suffered from an unceasing barrage of ailments and conditions–all somewhat related to congenital asthma which the family generically called *cholera morbus*. His little body was continually wracked by coughs, colds, nausea, and chronic diarrhea. His younger sister would later relate that "Rarely, even at his best, could he sleep without being propped up in bed or a big chair." [28] His gauntness and fragility reminded his mother of the pale withering azaleas of early summer. And it was whispered that he probably would not live to see his fourth birthday.

The return of his father from the war was a tonic to the whole family. And while Teedie took a turn for the better, he continued to suffer poor health throughout his childhood. He was often confined as an invalid for months at a time. And his earliest memories were of fitful nights gasping for a breath of air while both of his parents hovered about his sickbed.

During his long convalescences he benefited from the tales and reminiscences of his parents and grandparents. They would regale him with stories, legends, and songs from the past. They would fill his mind with florid romance, dashing adventure, and a fierce sense of his proud heritage that would ever after shape his consciousness. Later, he continued to feed his voracious appetite for such things, becoming a life-long avid reader.

His father, concerned that Teedie's sickly body would never allow him to enjoy the kind of full life he constantly read about, at last confronted him with the issue. "Theodore," the big man said, "you have the mind but you have not the body. And without the body the mind cannot go as far as it should. You must *make* your body. It is hard drudgery to make one's body, but I know you will do it." [29]

His mother later remembered her son's reaction was the half-grin, half-snarl which later became world famous. Jerking his head back, Teedie set his jaw and replied, "I'll make my body. By heaven, *I will.*" [30]

Indeed, he did. With bulldog tenacity he began to make daily visits to a local gym to lift weights, to box and spar, and to compete in gymnastic exercises. Later, he installed a small gym in the second-floor piazza off his bedroom, where he literally beat his body into submission.

PRECOCIOUS YOUTH

*While still a young boy I began to take an interest
in natural history. I remember distinctly the first day
that I started on my career as a zoologist.*[31]

*I*n further attempts to strengthen his frail son's body,
Theodore Senior began to take his family each
spring and summer to the rugged shores of Oyster Bay on
Long Island. There Teedie and the other children learned to
appreciate the joys of nature. They swam along the beach,
rode horses up and down the rolling hills, hiked through the
woods, hunted in the meadows, fished in the streams, and
rowed across the bay. They built wigwams at the edge of the
forest, gathered hickory nuts and wild apples, climbed to the
tops of the tallest trees, and scampered down long, leafy foot
trails.

Despite his incessant illness, Teedie seemed to have an
inexhaustible fund of energy. He could hardly be kept still–
even when sorely afflicted by one of his debilitating asthma
attacks. His many hours of enforced reading combined with his
keen powers of observation in the woods quickly combined to

make him something of a prodigy. He became a serious student of natural history–keeping detailed journals and notes of his sagacious studies of local flora and fauna. By age seven, he had begun a little museum containing a carefully indexed and classified collection of insects, bird nests, rocks, minerals, and cocoons. And by the time he was nine, his repertoire of specimens had expanded to snakes, rodents, birds, and small mammals. He even began to learn the technical processes of taxidermy.

When the family embarked on a year-long grand tour of Europe in 1869, Teedie's intellectual proclivities became particularly pronounced. He not only reveled in the art and architecture, history and pageantry, chivalry and nobility of the continent, he was fascinated by its spectacular natural beauty. From the dales of England to the forests of Germany, from the mountains of Switzerland to the valleys of the Rhine, from the highlands of Lombardy to the lowlands of Belgium, Teedie was bedazzled by the infinite variety of creation.

His diaries indicate a mind capable of astonishingly prodigious recall and insatiable appetites. Already, historian Edmund Morris points out, the contours of his interests and character were in evidence:

> *"Promptness, excitability, warmth, histrionics,*
> *love of plants and animals, physical vitality,*
> *dee-light, sensitivity to birdsong, fascination*
> *with military display, humor, family closeness,*
> *the conservationist, the historian, the hunter—*
> *all are here."*[32]

While Teedie attained marked intellectual growth, his conscience was also pricked by the poverty and deprivation he had witnessed abroad. His father was either the founder or an early supporter of virtually every cultural, humanitarian, and philanthropic endeavor in the city of New York. His unceasing efforts to establish the New York Orthopedic Hospital, the Children's Aid Society, and the Newsboys' Lodging House had already made a deep impression on his son. Theodore Senior was instrumental in organizing the Protective War Claims Association, the Soldiers' Employment Bureau, and the Blackwell's Island Sanitarium Society. The founding meetings of the American Museum of Natural History and the Metropolitan Museum of Art were both called by him and held in the family's front parlor. And he made certain that the life and fellowship of the Madison Square Presbyterian Church were central priorities for the family–not only on Sundays when he taught a mission class, but throughout the week. As a result, young Teedie had a ready context within which to develop his newly awakened concerns.

Toward the end of 1872, the Roosevelts embarked on yet another foreign adventure–one even more adventurous than their previous grand tour of Europe. In addition to long sojourns in England, Germany, and Italy, they visited the Middle East–including Palestine, Syria, and Egypt. It was on this trip that all of the disparate aspects of Teedie's wide-ranging interests–books, history, scientific observation, the outdoor life, and Christian social concern–began to be fully integrated into a cohesive worldview. As his father related, "He went away a boy and returned a young man." [33]

THE HARVARD DANDY

*I thoroughly enjoyed Harvard and I am sure it did
me good, but only in the general effect, for there was
very little in my actual studies which helped me in
after life.*[34]

*H*omeschooled by his very capable Bulloch aunt,
Teedie had gained a rich classical education–
studying the sundry general liberal arts of literature, history,
music, theology, and philosophy, the venerable Trivium disciplines of Grammar, Logic, and Rhetoric, as well as the various
Quadrivium derivatives of German, French, Astronomy, Bio-
logy, Architecture, and Geometry. By the time he was fifteen,
he was well versed in the Western Canon of classical literature–from the golden age of Pagan Antiquity to the glorious
flowering of Christendom, and from the precipitous dawning
of the Reformation to the ominous disconsonance of the
Enlightenment. He was particularly knowledgeable in the area
of military and political biography–he drank deeply from the
wells of Virgil, Plutarch, Augustine, Cato, Athanasius, Eusebius,
Seneca, Machiavelli, Johnson, Burke, Carlyle, and Macaulay.

Despite this great breadth and depth of intellectual acumen, he was sorely deficient in several areas of great importance. If he were to be admitted to Harvard–where he longed to pursue his interests in natural science and history–he would have to vastly improve his skills in Greek, Latin, and Mathematics. A tutor was secured for this purpose and just as he had determinedly set out to "make his body," he now focused on "making his mind."

In 1876 he passed the rigorous entrance exams and enrolled in the prestigious school. His father sent him off with the sage counsel, "Take care of your morals first, your health next, and finally your studies." [35] He did just that.

Though he tackled a full academic course load, he immediately engaged himself in a number of extra-curricular activities designed to fulfill the greatest hopes and expectations of his parents. He taught a Sunday School class at Christ Episcopal Church in Cambridge. He began to publish a series of serious articles on various scientific, social, and political subjects. He became an avid participant in the school's intramural athletics program. And he joined the Rifle Club, the Natural History Club, the Finance Club, as well as the elite Porcellian Club. He also nurtured a wide range of social relations–thus establishing friendships he would maintain throughout his life and career.

Though he was considered by his classmates as a dandy and a raconteur because of his stylish dress and confident demeanor, he was anything but. In fact, everything he was and everything he did was animated by his devotion to his family and by his determination to maintain their esteem. He told his mother that because of them, "I have never spent an unhappy day unless by my own fault." [36] And he wrote his father saying, "I do not think there is a fellow in College who has a family who love him as much as you all do me. I am sure that there is no one who has a father who is also his best and most intimate friend, as you are mine. I have kept the first letter you wrote me and shall do my best to deserve your trust." [37]

Sadly, his blissful existence was to be shattered during the winter term of his second year at Harvard. His father, though only forty-six and always a paragon of vim, vigor, and vitality, was stricken with what was diagnosed as acute peritonitis–but which was actually a virulent strain of stomach cancer. In less than two months he was dead.

Suddenly called home from school, Teedie found the entire city in mourning–with flags flown at half mast and black bunting draped across the crenelations of the public buildings. Lauded in the *Harper's Weekly,* Roosevelt Senior was described as an "American citizen of the best type–cheerful, hearty, sagacious, honest, hopeful; not to be swerved by abuse, by hostility, or by derision." His father was sorely missed by all who knew him. Though inconsolably stricken with grief, young Roosevelt, as the eldest son, had to act the part of the head of the house.

When he returned to school following the funeral, he was determined more than ever to uphold the honor of his name. "How I wish I could ever do something to keep up his name." [38] To that end, he vowed to "study well, finish Harvard, and carry on like a brave Christian gentleman." [39]

FAIRY TALE LOVE

There is no joy that hurts so well as young love. [40]

*T*he next summer, young Roosevelt's relationship with Edith Carrow blossomed into a serious romance. Playmates, best friends, and sweethearts since they were toddlers, no one was surprised when they became all but inseparable. They went rowing, sailing, hiking, and picnicking together. By all accounts they were perfect for one another–not only sharing a passionate interest in books, ideas, science, and charitable concerns, but balancing one another's temperaments: where he was "ardent and impulsive, feverish in his enthusiasms, she was sensitive and cautious, a cooling breeze over his sometimes overheated landscape." [41]

But then one afternoon they apparently quarreled bitterly. They broke off their relationship in a fit of fury–and would hardly see one another for years afterward. Brokenhearted, Roosevelt returned to Harvard.

Less than two months later though, he met another beautiful young lady–and suddenly all rueful thoughts of Edith's lost love were banished. Alice Lee was the seventeen-year-old

daughter of a prominent Boston banking family. Fair, flirta-
tious, radiant, and vivacious, Alice was quite popular with the
privileged sons of New England gentry, as well as the bright
young men of Harvard. But from the moment he laid his eyes
on her, Roosevelt would countenance no challenge to his
determination to "marry that girl." [42]

With all the ardor that seemed to attend everything he
undertook in life, Roosevelt began to court Alice. During the
next weeks and months, he used all of his considerable
charms to win her heart–though he recorded in his diary that
he had "asked God's help in staving off temptation and to do
nothing" that he "would have been ashamed to confess" to his
father. [43]

Amazingly, he was able to maintain his excellent grades–
and in his senior year he juggled his relentless pursuit of
Alice with his many extra-curricular activities. He was elected
to the Hasty Pudding Club. He was asked to preside over the
Finance and Natural History Clubs. He vied for the light-
weight boxing championship–ultimately winning the silver
medal. And he had begun an ambitious project of writing an
authoritative book about the naval history of the War of 1812.

Though she resisted for some time, in the end, Alice was
won over completely by his boundless energies, enthusiasms,
and affections. On January 25, 1880, she consented to marry
him. Roosevelt was ecstatic. The final semester whirled past
as he made joyous preparations for their new life together.

There was, however, one dark cloud hanging over his
happy existence. And he told no one about it–not even his
beloved Alice–until the very end of his life. Shortly before
graduation, he had a complete physical examination. The
results were alarming. The doctor had detected a frighten-
ingly erratic heartbeat and warned the young man to choose
a sedentary occupation–he even advised him to avoid all

physical exercise including going up and down stairs if he wished to enjoy a long life.

Typically, Roosevelt quickly retorted, "Doctor, I am going to do all the things you've told me not to. If I must live the sort of life you have described, I don't care how short it is." [44] Shortly afterward, he emphasized his resolve by mountain climbing in Maine. Then later that summer, he embarked on an exhausting six-week hunting expedition to the West with his younger brother.

On October 27, 1880, he married his "sweet, blue-eyed queen" Alice. At the reception following the simple ceremony, the sunshine, champagne, and merriment generated such euphoria that even Edith Carrow–who of all the guests had the least reason to celebrate–happily "danced the soles off her shoes." [45] For once the verbose Roosevelt was utterly speechless in the thrall of his fairy tale romance. He noted tersely in his diary that, "Our intense happiness is too sacred to be written about." [46]

A REFORMER'S ZEAL

*What is politics for if not to right wrongs and to
stand for truth?*[47]

*A*fter a brief honeymoon at Oyster Bay, the newly-
weds settled in New York where Roosevelt had
enrolled at the prestigious Columbia University Law School.
He was still somewhat uncertain about his future, but he had
determined that whatever course he might eventually take, a
study of the law would prove to be beneficial.

He plunged into his studies with his usual fervor, but
quickly found he needed more of a challenge than his profes-
sors could provide. So each afternoon following a full
schedule of classes he would plunge into his research and
writing for *The Naval War of 1812.* Upon publication, the
book was immediately heralded as a "formidable literary
achievement" [48] and the "harbinger of a great new historical
talent." [49] This was indeed remarkable–especially considering
its author was a mere twenty-three years old and had begun
the project while still an undergraduate. A century after its
first appearance, *The Naval War of 1812* remains a standard

work on the subject on both sides of the Atlantic–and a required text at the United States Naval Academy.

Meanwhile his romance with Alice continued unabated. They enjoyed a wide circle of friends and were quickly swept into a swirl of social engagements. Roosevelt was only too happy to show off his beautiful wife. With his scintillating and controversial mind and her stunning and gracious presence, they became the talk of the town in no time.

With the acclaim that attended the successful launch of his publishing career and the attention that accompanied his stellar social rise, came the interested scrutiny of various political forces within the city. Indeed, Roosevelt had already involved himself in various local controversies and had become an active member of his neighborhood Republican Club–making his mark as an unabashed advocate of political reform. It was probably inevitable that opportunity-seeking reformers in the corrupt, machine-dominated city should put his name forward as a possible candidate for the state Assembly. Tired of the party establishment's incessant back room wheeling and dealing, the delegates at his precinct caucus surprisingly disregarded the experienced incumbent and nominated the young upstart in 1882.

Not long afterward, Roosevelt outlined his political philosophy in his journal, writing that he would be a "strong Republican on state matters, but an Independent on municipal matters." [50] Thus, at the very beginning of his career, he signaled a principled tension between party loyalty on the one hand and singular independence on the other–a tension that was to dominate his life in politics ever after.

Much to the alarm of his backers, he had a tendency to speak his mind. Nevertheless, his constituency found his honesty a refreshing departure from politics as usual. He won easily–becoming the youngest member of the New York Assembly.

As historian Nathan Miller has observed, "Theodore Roosevelt burst upon Albany with the same effect he had at Harvard and within a few months became one of the most prominent figures in New York politics." [51] He delivered his maiden speech a few days after arriving at the capital. The Assembly was deadlocked concerning the competing claims of two Democratic rivals for the speakership. Upon learning that several Republicans were discussing the possibility of throwing their support to one or the other in order to expedite the business of government, Roosevelt leapt to his feet to object on the grounds that it was good politics to let the Democrats tear themselves apart. "As things are today in New York, there are two branches of Jeffersonian Democrats," he declared. "Neither of these alone can carry the state against the Republicans. Clearly then, we have no interest in helping one section against the other." He went on to assert, "While in New York City, I talked with several gentlemen who have large commercial interests at stake. They do not seem to care whether the deadlock is broken or not. In fact, they seem rather relieved. And if we do no business until the end of the session, I think the voters of the state get along quite well without it." [52]

The press lauded his combination of brash conservatism and reformist zeal as "the most refreshing new development in New York politics in decades" and "the voice of a new era in American statesmanship." [53] And thus, a star was born.

During the next several months, Roosevelt led an odd coalition of mugwumps, progressives, and reform-minded conservatives in a firebrand crusade to clean up the state's corrupt judicial and civil service spoils systems. There was much at stake–vast wealth and tremendous power was wielded by the entrenched political bosses. Not surprisingly then, virtually none of the pundits or prognosticators of the day gave Roosevelt any real chance of success. Though they privately may have admired his brave attempt to restore civic virtue, they publicly derided it as little more than an idealistic and quixotic quest, doomed to failure.

Nevertheless, despite his youthful inexperience, lack of any substantive political base, and innumerable threats against his life and well-being, the sheer force of his energy, courage, and tenacity somehow secured one legislative victory after another. Though the changes he had wrought were modest, he had suddenly come to symbolize the hope of reformers everywhere.

Again and again Roosevelt declared his political credo was simply "to take out of politics the vast band of hired mercenaries whose very existence depends on their success, and who can almost always overcome the efforts of them whose only care is to secure pure and honest government." [54] It was not exactly the kind of credo designed to win over the confidence of the political establishment. But it did gain for him a faithful following among the masses–a following that would remain dedicated to him throughout his long career. During the next two election cycles, his constituents rewarded his integrity and selfless courage with the widest re-election margins of any legislator in New York.

TRAGEDY

*Life brings sorrows and joys alike. It is what a man
does with them–not what they do to him–that is the
true test of his mettle.*[55]

Some three years after their marriage, Alice finally
became pregnant. Roosevelt was thrilled. He desperately wanted children–longing to create for them the kind
of family life he had enjoyed as a child. Alice, too, was
delighted.

Immediately they both turned their attentions to the
house they planned to build on a grassy hilltop overlooking
Oyster Bay on Long Island. Roosevelt had already purchased
nearly a hundred acres there and had engaged architects to
design a "spacious home with a multitude of gables, dormers,
windows, chimneys, and a sprawling wrap-around porch"
where he and Alice and their brood of children could sit on
rocking chairs and contemplate the sunset.[56] With ten bed-
rooms, a comfortable gentleman's library, and facilities for
gracious entertainment, the house was to be a quite a grand
endeavor–well beyond the means of the young couple. But

then Roosevelt rarely tackled a project that was sensibly within his means.

Distracted by the call of duty back in Albany, Roosevelt was forced to leave Alice several times during her pregnancy–much to the distress of both of them. Each day he would write tender letters to her expressing his deepest affections:

"I have to read my Bible all to myself, without my pretty queenie standing beside me in front of the looking glass combing out her hair. There is no pretty, sleeping rosebud face to kiss and love when I wake in the morning." [57]

Despite the joyous anticipation of his first born, he was deeply concerned for his delicate wife. And for good reason. Alice was not having an easy time of it. Because of her frail constitution she was forced to spend much of the pregnancy in bed. All of the regular distresses of child-bearing–from nausea and swelling in the joints to back pains and severe abdominal cramping–were magnified for her.

When she went into labor prematurely, Roosevelt was away at the capital. Happily though, on February 12, 1884, Alice safely delivered a healthy eight-and three-quarter-pound baby girl.

But then the real trouble began. The telegram sent to Roosevelt the next morning noted that while the baby was in good health, the mother was "only fairly well." A few hours later, he received another message ominously bidding him to return to New York "immediately." [58]

When at last he reached home, he was met by his distraught brother with dire words: "There is a curse on this house. Mother is dying and Alice is dying too." [59] The doctors had diagnosed Alice as suffering from Bright's Disease–a severe renal ailment, which had gone undetected throughout her pregnancy. Martha Bulloch Roosevelt, who had fallen ill with what appeared to be a cold a few days before, was diagnosed as suffering from the final stages of typhoid. The two people dearest to him in all the world were now on the threshold of death–at the same time in the same house.

Roosevelt rushed up the stairs and disconsolately held Alice in his arms for several hours while she hung on to life by a slender thread. He was beckoned downstairs where his mother was drawing her final breaths. Sometime after midnight, she died, and Roosevelt ran back up the stairs to Alice. His vigil continued through the long night and into the next afternoon, when at last, Alice too died. It was St. Valentine's Day. Alice was just twenty-two years old.

Two days later, Roosevelt sat in the front pew of the Fifth Avenue Presbyterian Church–where he and Alice had worshipped together so many times–for the double funeral. The next day, they were back in the same pew for the baptism of Roosevelt's little daughter. She was christened Alice Lee.

Later he would write in his journal, "The light has gone out of my life." [60]

GO WEST YOUNG MAN

*In after years there shall ever come to mind the
memory of endless prairies shimmering in the bright
sun; of vast, snow-clad wastes, lying desolate under
gray skies; of the melancholy marshes; of the rush of
mighty rivers; of the breath of the evergreen forest in
summer; of the crooning of ice-armored pines at the
touch of the winds of winter; of cataracts roaring
between hoary mountain passes; of all the innumerable sights and sounds of the wilderness and of the
silences that brood in its still depths.*[61]

*T*he shock of his tragic loss, as well as a series of disconcerting political machinations within the
Republican party, combined to entirely demoralize Roosevelt.
Reevaluating all of his priorities, he resolved to leave his old
life in New York behind and make a career out west in the
wide open ranges of the Dakota Territories. Leaving his infant
daughter with his sister, he sold off most of his possessions
and departed for his season in the wilderness–both literally
and figuratively.

During the previous two years he had been cautiously

investing a portion of his inheritance from his father in a cattle ranch overlooking a bend in the Little Missouri River. With a couple of his old hunting and tracking cronies from Maine, he decided to manage his investment on site.

Though he could not have known it at the time, it may well have been the most astute political decision he had ever made–or ever would. Historian Nathan Miller has asserted that

> *Roosevelt had three major liabilities in politics: he was an aristocrat, he was an intellectual, and he was an easterner. Altogether, he spent only about three years in the Badlands, a period interrupted by sometimes lengthy stays in the East. Yet he so successfully identified himself with the West that for the remainder of his life, the public thought of him as a rough-riding cowboy rather than a New York dude. This western experience removed the stigma of effeminacy, ineffectuality, and intellectualism that clung to most reformers.*[62]

Even so, his move out West was anything but image-conscious posturing. He had every intention of staying there for the rest of his life. And in short order, Roosevelt won the respect of the rough and tumble men of the frontier range by his unflinching courage, his unfailing honesty, and his unfettered enthusiasm for the land. Sometimes with his fists, sometimes with his gun, but most often with his cunning, he carved out a new and satisfying life for himself among them. In addition, he was a quick study and gained their approval as a skilled rancher.

His long arduous days on the cattle trail were often followed by equally long and arduous nights with pen and paper. Roosevelt turned his many western adventures into a series of well-received books–including *Hunting Trips of a Ranchman, Ranch Life and the Hunting Trail, The Wilderness Hunter,* and a biography of the western expansionist, *Thomas Hart Benton.*

Reviewers lauded the works as "masculine, fervid, and innovative." [63] Indeed, the books sparked a whole new interest in the issues of the range and the lifestyle of the rugged frontiersman. They dramatically brought the world of the rancher to life with vivid descriptions of the land, the people, and its wildlife. They essentially created a whole new genre of literature. With the novels of his old friend and Harvard classmate, Owen Wister, and the art of Frederic Remington, his books helped to generate the great American legend and lore of the "Wild West."

Of course, the wildness of the West was not simply legend and lore. Roosevelt alone had enough genuine adventures with bucking broncos, grizzly bears, and desperadoes to certify it as such.

In one his most famous escapades, Roosevelt tracked two petty thieves for three days across more than a hundred miles of wilderness. Battered by a howling wind and subzero temperatures, he nevertheless brought them to justice–traveling another six days and 150 miles downstream to do so.

Now it appeared he was a genuine American hero and not a "pasteboard figure made by the artifice of politics and wealth." [64]

DESTINY FULFILLED

*Happy homes are the responsibility of husbands and
fathers–but inevitably it is wives and mothers who
make it so.*[65]

When he at last returned to New York, his friends
and acquaintances were amazed by his dra-
matic transformation. It was almost as if his lifelong struggle
against illness and frailty, as well as his more recent struggle
against grief and despair, were suddenly crowned with an
unexpected victory. The anemic and dispirited dandy who had
left the city had returned rugged, bronzed, and in the prime
of health.

Indeed, his whole demeanor was changed. According to
one observer, "There was very little of the whilom dude in his
rough and easy carriage." [66] Even his crisp, clipped New York
accent had been smoothed into the easier, relaxed tones of the
frontier. His old friend William Thayer, who had not seen him
for several years, was astonished "to find him with the neck
of a Titan and with broad shoulders and a stalwart chest." [67]
He speculated that "this magnificent specimen of manhood"

would have to spend the rest of his life "struggling to reconcile the conflicting demands of a powerful mind and an equally powerful body." [68]

One day shortly after his conspicuous return, he met Edith Carrow coming down the stairs of his sister's house. For nearly seven years, he had managed to almost completely avoid her. But his childhood sweetheart had remained his sister's closest friend–and while he was away she had been a regular visitor in the Roosevelt household.

He now discovered that in the intervening years, she had become alarmingly attractive. Rejecting any and all potential suitors–at the risk of becoming an old maid–she had matured into a complex figure of femininity and loveliness.

Against his will, he was utterly smitten.

During the next several weeks they began to see more and more of each other. Though driven by a sense of guilt–he somehow believed that he was being untrue to the memory of Alice–Roosevelt asked Edith to marry him. She accepted without hesitation–she had always loved him and no other.

After a quick trip back to his ranch to settle a few business affairs, he now returned to the East to stay. His original plan was to attempt to make a living with his scientific writing and journalism. But politics would simply not leave him alone.

No sooner had he unpacked his bags than several influential New York Republicans urged him to accept the party's nomination for mayor. There was little chance of winning–the election was a mere three weeks away and had already attracted two other well-financed candidates. But they believed that the young Roosevelt could make a strong showing, thus establishing a precedent for the borough balloting to be held later in the year.

Roosevelt accepted the challenge and entered the fray with his usual enthusiasm. Known as the "Cowboy Candidate," he worked eighteen-hour days, appeared at four or five rallies every night, and won over the city's typically jaded media. Indeed, the *New York Times* exuded, "He excites more confidence and enthusiasm than has been inspired by any candidate in a mayoralty contest within the memory of this generation of voters." [69]

In the end, though he had surprisingly made a real race out of it, Roosevelt was defeated. His heroic last-minute stumping was simply too little, too late–though he had certainly proven his popular appeal to the power-brokers and king-makers in the party establishment.

A few days later, Roosevelt, his sister, and Edith boarded a steamer and set sail across the Atlantic. The couple would fulfill what each of them believed to be their providential destiny.

On December 2, 1886, Theodore Roosevelt and Edith Carrow were married in a quiet, private ceremony at St. George's Church, Hanover Square, in London.

A POLITICAL QUEST

The worst enemies of the republic are the dema-
gogue and the corruptionist.[70]

*F*ollowing a leisurely honeymoon in Europe, the
Roosevelts moved into the newly completed but
never-inhabited house at Oyster Bay–now dubbed Sagamore
Hill. Believing his political career now to be finished for all
intents and purposes, Roosevelt turned his energy toward
establishing his literary reputation.

First, he wrote a fine biography of Gouverneur Morris,
the mastermind behind the first draft of the Constitution. The
book was remarkable for its clarity of vision and its applicability to the contemporary political scene. Roosevelt obviously
had that essential conservative trait of being able to find
immediate lessons for the present from the past.

He also began work on a masterful multi-volume history
entitled *The Winning of the West.* It was to be a sweeping
drama of the heroism, hardship, warfare, and struggle that
made the conquest of the North American continent not only
possible, but inevitable.

He dug deeply into original sources and his research was meticulous–although he completely rejected the modern German-inspired notion of academic history as a kind of social science. Instead it was a branch of literature. "History," he argued, "should be a work of art and imagination rather than a dry compendium of facts." [71] He was an unashamed moralist who whole-heartedly believed that it was the duty of the historian to make value judgments to draw immediate and applicable lessons for the contemporary reader. The result was a remarkably fresh perspective of the American story–one as vibrant as the events themselves.

The books received rave reviews; it appeared he would indeed be able to support his growing family–Edith had five children in quick succession during the next few years–with his pen.

Once again though, Roosevelt's quiet respite from the hubbub of politics was short-lived. When Republican Benjamin Harrison won the presidency in 1888, he was tapped to fill one of three Civil Service Commission positions in the new administration.

Roosevelt gave his all in all to this rather unglamorous but vitally important position. Before long, he had transformed the sleepy little department into the locus of reform in the federal government. Once again, it was Roosevelt against the forces of corruption, recalcitrance, and cronyism–only this time, it was a part of his job description. He was charged by the new president to completely restructure the way jobs in the vast federal bureaucracy were doled out.

Always a skilled tactician, he was careful to fulfill that mandate while at the same time keeping the ruling coalition intact and in charge. And that was no mean feat. For years the spoils system had been the means by which politicians paid their debts to supporters–rather than making appointments based on any system of merit. Thus, cushy federal offices had become the corrupt currency of political life. Obviously, there were entrenched forces determined that their vested interests were left undisturbed. That meant Roosevelt had to face off against some of the most ruthless men in the country. He thought that sounded "just bully." [72]

For the next four years, his efforts catapulted the dull cause of civil service reform onto the front pages of the newspapers–and propelled Roosevelt into the national limelight. In fact, he became such a powerful and popular voice for government integrity and efficiency that when the Republicans lost power in the next election, the new Democratic administration wisely decided that they could ill afford to replace him. He was the only Republican office holder to be so retained.

Though flattered by the new administration's recognition of his accomplishments, Roosevelt no longer felt challenged by the job. So when the opportunity arose to take the job of New York City's police commissioner, he jumped at the chance.

Once again, he was cast in the role of a reformer. This time, instead of trying to manage the vast federal bureaucracy, he was to rid the nation's largest and most important police department of graft, corruption, and inefficiency–and there was plenty "to get rid of." [73]

A sullen indolence had come to dominate the force. The department was run as a kind of personal fiefdom by the political machine in the city. Officers were "on the take" in virtually every borough. Prostitution rings, gambling cartels, drug smuggling cabals, and protection rackets operated with impunity.

He quickly modernized the entire system of operations–introducing such innovations as forensics, fingerprinting, rap sheets, and investigative departments–thus pioneering standard police procedures that have remained in use to this day.

He walked the beats himself–often alone at night–in an effort to catch officers who were sleeping on the job, shaking down the citizenry, or engaging in other illegal activities. He restructured the entire chain of command and instituted a system of merit that completely altered the character of the criminal justice system around the nation.

His phenomenal successes once again thrust him into the national limelight. Though he was only thirty-seven years old, his name was often mentioned in connection with the presidency. His star was definitely on the rise.

Meanwhile, despite such a flurry of public activity, Roosevelt had settled into an immensely happy family life. He was by all accounts an ideal father. His children adored him– and he gave himself to them with complete abandon. Edith often complained that she actually had seven children to contend with–not six. But he was also a devoted husband. Not only did he remain head over heels in love with her, he was careful to keep their relationship his first priority–even amidst so many other pressing responsibilities.

Given his incredible public productivity and his private penchants, one New York socialite quipped with no little exasperation, "How can anyone possibly be that perfect? Surely there is dirt under the corner of the carpet somewhere." Edith quickly responded, "Not a speck." [74]

Rough Rider

There is nothing more for me to do here in
Washington. I've got to go into the fight myself.[75]

*T*he next national elections brought the Republicans
to power once again and Roosevelt yearned for a
strategic appointment that would enable him to do more than
simply clean up the messes others had made. He wanted to
be a constructive reformer rather than always being cast in
the role of a critical reformer.

Ever since writing *The Naval War of 1812*, he had been
an advocate of building a strong navy–a stance that had not
been incorporated into American defensive strategy since the
War between the States. In addition, he had become increas-
ingly convinced that a showdown was imminent between the
old colonial powers of Europe and the United States. Thus, he
sought for an appointment as undersecretary of the Navy. His
rationale was simple: "I want to be where the action is."[76]

After a brief hesitation–President McKinley's advisors
were somewhat cautious about Roosevelt's independent
streak–he won his coveted prize and went to work with all his

typical ardor. He quickly mastered the technical details of running a modern navy and became an expert in everything from munitions and armor plating to blast trajectories and fuel efficiency ratings. His boss, the former governor of Massachusetts, John Long, was entirely uninterested in such details. That suited Roosevelt. After all, that meant he was essentially left to run the Navy as he saw fit–within congressional guidelines, of course.

At the time, the naval fleet was a small, uncoordinated, and dilapidated force that served as little more than a ceremonial coast guard. It ranked well behind the navies of Britain, France, Germany, Spain, Russia, and Japan–with only four first-class battleships, two armored cruisers, and forty-eight other vessels of various types, ranging from harbor tug boats to small torpedo launches. Roosevelt embarked on an aggressive campaign to expand and modernize the fleet. He also drew up strategic plans to better coordinate the resources already at hand should war come with one of the great powers.

And he was convinced that it would come. He was particularly concerned about Spain. The old colonial behemoth was engaged in quashing rebellions all across its wide-flung empire–in the Philippines, in Puerto Rico, and most seriously, in Cuba. Reports of fierce oppression had stirred American public opinion against the Spanish, and administration concerns about the obstruction of international commerce had rankled the ire of Congress. Thus, Roosevelt readied his department as best he could for what he was convinced would be a nasty confrontation.

As it turned out, Roosevelt's instincts were all too prescient. He had secured the promotion of Commodore George Dewey to commander of the Asiatic Squadron, supplied him with a strategy for the conquest of Manila Bay, and placed him on war readiness. Similarly, he outlined a Caribbean strategy that would isolate Spanish interests and bring independence to Cuba.

President McKinley–cautious as always–wanted to avoid the pretext for war at all costs. Thus, he ordered a large armored cruiser, the *Maine*, to make a "courtesy visit" to Havana from Key West, its port of call. A few weeks later, while the Maine lay peacefully at anchor in the harbor at Havana, an explosion ripped through the hull of the American vessel. Casualties were heavy–266 of the 354 crew members were killed. Although an investigation of the blast failed to reveal direct Spanish complicity, war now seemed inevitable.

Roosevelt's mobilization plans were quickly implemented–and ultimately proved to be the decisive difference in the war. Meanwhile, he had resigned his position with the Navy after winning a commission to command a volunteer detachment of troopers on the front lines of battle.

Everyone who knew him tried to dissuade him from what appeared to be a foolhardy and unnecessary risk. Even President McKinley argued that his influence would be greater if he would stay in Washington. As if that were not enough, Edith was recovering from a life-threatening illness–and he had his own troop of six children at home to care for.

But nothing could keep him away from the action. "If I am to be any use in politics, " he said, "it is because I am supposed to be a man who does not preach what he fears to practice. For the last year I have preached war with Spain. I should feel distinctly ashamed if I now failed to practice what I have preached." [77]

The regiment Colonel Roosevelt was to command was composed of a thousand men–some Eastern dandies, some Western cowboys, and only a handful of experienced soldiers. Nevertheless, they were whipped into fighting shape quickly–

at a camp near San Antonio, Texas–and shipped to the front lines. In less than a month and a half Roosevelt had taken them from raw recruits to an efficient fighting force.

On June 22, 1898, the Rough Riders–as they had been dubbed by the popular press–landed on the pristine beaches some twenty miles from the strategic city of Santiago. In short order they were involved in several fierce fire-fights with the seasoned Spanish defenders. Movement was treacherous and slow. Even so, Roosevelt demonstrated coolness and bravery under fire and quickly earned the respect of his men. He advanced his corps over the next several days toward Santiago. On July 1, they were in position for a charge up the last hill for a final assault on the heavily fortified Spanish garrison.

Like Shakespeare's Henry V before the Battle of Agincourt, Roosevelt moved among his men, lending them hearty encouragement and checking on last-minute contingencies. For as long as he lived, he looked back on that day as "the greatest of my life." [78] And it was indeed glorious. The assault was successful. Casualties, though heavy, were fewer than expected.

Roosevelt was no less heroic after the great battle than he was during it. He seemed everywhere–securing essential provisions, opening direct communications for officers back home, coordinating the inefficient quartermastering, and maintaining high morale among the enlisted men. And he even secured early release of the troops once the Spanish crown had officially capitulated. He seemed to cast a spell of reverence and awe wherever he went.

The commander of the overall operation, General Joseph Wheeler, recognized Roosevelt's vital role in the victory and recommended him for the Medal of Honor. But the people of the United States accorded him an even greater honor–they garnered him with universal praise and adulation. Only thirty-nine years old, Colonel Theodore Roosevelt, commander of the Rough Riders, was now the most famous, the most admired, and the most popular man in America–bar none.

A POLITICAL ACCIDENT

We worked very hard; but I made a point of getting a couple of hours off each day for equally vigorous play.[79]

*R*oosevelt returned home to discover a bevy of political opportunists seeking his favor and attention. A group of independent reformers, progressives, and mugwumps wanted him to consider starting a national third-party movement. A group of influential Republicans desired him to run for Congress. Another group wanted him to run for governor. Still another group wanted him to consider challenging the Republican presidential nomination.

Weighing his options carefully, he decided the wisest course for the present was to seek the gubernatorial prize. His closest friend and political advisor, Henry Cabot Lodge, concurred. If his goal was eventually to reach the White House, there was no better stepping stone than the Governor's Mansion in Albany–five of the seven presidential races since the War between the States had featured either a sitting governor or a former governor from the state.

Campaigning on a simple platform of "courage," an "upright judiciary," and "honesty in government," Roosevelt captured the moral high ground early in the contest. The result was never in doubt.

In keeping with his view of limited government and principled conservatism, his administration was most noted for its efforts to bring about bureaucratic efficiency, managerial economy, tax reform, and meritorial advancement in the civil service. He continually appealed for practical morality and manly virtue in the civic arena. "It is absolutely impossible," he declared, "for a Republic long to endure if it becomes either corrupt or cowardly." [80]

His accomplishments as governor were impressive. They included banning local option segregation of schools, securing the rights of workers to choose whether or not to unionize, bringing about sweeping municipal reform to New York City, and establishing the first state-wide tax reform code banning property seizures without jury trials.

As always, he was a hive of activity in his private life–and he had a knack for keeping himself in the public eye even when he stepped away from his official duties. He wrote a bevy of articles and books. He gave an enormous number of speeches. He traveled to every corner of the state. He kept the pace of his outdoors activities and his scientific endeavors. He remained faithfully involved in his local church–still teaching in his Sunday School class as often as possible. And of course, he plunged headlong into the myriad activities of his bustling young family.

Not surprisingly, when the vice president, Garret Hobart, died unexpectedly, a ground-swell of support from all across the nation put Roosevelt's name at the top of the list of candidates to replace him on the Republican ticket for 1900. Though President William McKinley was cool to the idea at first–again, fearing Roosevelt's impetuously independent streak–he at last consented.

It was a good thing he did, too. The Republican convention that summer was like a coronation party for Roosevelt. As the center of attention, he was actually quite resistant to the notion of becoming vice president. He was afraid it was a political dead end rather than the opportunity of a lifetime. In fact, several of his fiercest rivals supported the idea of placing him on the ticket because they believed it would sufficiently sidetrack his career and keep him safely away from the action.

But the delegates at the convention would not entertain Roosevelt's objections, and he was nominated unanimously on the first ballot.

President McKinley chose a front-porch campaign strategy–he did not venture out to even a single rally, assembly, or meeting during the race. Thus, the full weight of the election stumping was left to Roosevelt. Once again, his boundless energies and unflagging enthusiasms served him well. He gave hundreds of speeches and traversed nearly 25,000 miles. According to the press, the real story of the campaign could be adequately summed up in the words of a popular ditty: "Tis Teddy alone that's running, and he ain't just running, he's galloping." [81]

In the end, the Republicans won their greatest victory since the time of Reconstruction.

Roosevelt, despite the great role he had played in the election victory, was rather despondent once the dust had settled. "The Vice President is really a fifth wheel to the coach," he groused. "It is not a stepping stone to anything but oblivion." [82] In fact, his service in the active part of his new office lasted only four days.

During the summer congressional recess, he took advantage of the opportunity to spend some time at Sagamore Hill, go hunting, fishing, hiking, and climbing with his family in New England, and catch up on his reading–during the campaign he had drastically cut down his reading to a mere three or four books a week. He made a point to simply enjoy life to the fullest.

At the end of the summer President McKinley was winding up a two-day visit to the Pan American Exposition in Buffalo, New York. It was a lavish world's fair that dramatized the great cultural, scientific, economic, and industrial strides American had taken in the previous century.

President McKinley was greeting well-wishers in a reception line when a young anarchist stepped out of the crowd and shot him at point-blank range. Roosevelt rushed to his bedside; for the first several days it appeared he might well recover. By September 10, four days after the shooting, he seemed to be entirely out of danger and Roosevelt was told his departure from Buffalo would help assure the nation that the crisis was finished. But then on September 13, McKinley suddenly took a turn for the worse. Within twenty-four hours he was dead.

At the time, Roosevelt was climbing the remote Mount Marcy–the highest peak in the Adirondacks–with several close friends. They were on their way down from the exhausting climb when they were intercepted by a park ranger with the news. The men quickly hiked to the nearest telephone– about a dozen miles away–where they picked up a security detachment and a buckboard for the forty-mile ride to the nearest train station.

Somber and apparently lost in his thoughts, he barely spoke to anyone during the arduous journey. His train was mobbed by newsmen all along the way–but he remained in seclusion. He did not comment, in fact, until after he had taken the oath of office in Buffalo. Then he simply asserted:

*The administration of the government will not
falter in spite of the terrible blow. It shall be my
aim to continue, absolutely, unbroken, the
legacy of President McKinley for the peace,
the prosperity, and the honor of our beloved
country.*[83]

At forty-two, Theodore Roosevelt was now the youngest
president in American history. And though he had arrived at
the White House by accident, he had indeed arrived.

TR: REX

No man ever enjoyed being president more than I did.[84]

*T*heodore Roosevelt was born to be president of the United States. Once the American citizenry had recovered from the shock of the assassination, his presence in the White House seemed somehow natural, comfortable, even inevitable. He exuded a charismatic confidence that immediately set men at ease.

Nearly everything he did seemed to break new ground–and yet his progressive innovations and reforms all naturally grew out of his fiercely conservative Christian principles. He created a brouhaha when he invited the famed educator Booker T. Washington to the White House for dinner–the first Black to have such a privilege. He mandated equal pay for equal work in all federal offices–the first legal protection for female workers. He ordered the Justice Department to investigate any violations of the Sherman Anti-Trust Act–passed in 1890, but never consistently enforced. And, he announced to the colonial powers that he would forcefully prosecute any territorial encroachments under the authority of the Monroe Doctrine–again, long before enunciated but never before enforced.

In short, Roosevelt determined that at least with his administration, "The government should simply say what it means and mean what it says." [85] The public endorsed his program of honest government and the rule of law with solid Republican victories in the mid-term elections of 1902. His influence from the "bully pulpit" of the White House was felt far and wide.

As historian Nathan Miller noted:

> *In little more than a year in office, Roosevelt*
> *had captured the imagination of the American*
> *people. He had launched the Square Deal, bran-*
> *dished the Big Stick against the trusts,*
> *personally settled a major coal strike and won*
> *the support of labor and the public, enlarged*
> *the power and prestige of his office, and*
> *emerged as the leader of the Republican party.*
> *He had shown the will and skill to capitalize*
> *on the opportunities that came his way.* [86]

During the next two years leading up to the 1904 elections, Roosevelt continued to cement his mythic status. By negotiating the end of the devastating Russo-Japanese War, he not only became the first American to win the Nobel Peace Prize, but also established the United States as a genuine international power and an arbiter of peace. Many had feared that his course of military preparedness and aggressive stance on foreign affairs would inevitably lead America down the path of war; instead, his was the most conflict-free administration in history. Not a single shot was fired against a foreign foe and not a single engagement was seriously threatened at any time during his seven and a half years in office–though there were a few tense moments about European debt collection in revolution-wracked Venezuela, the acquisition of the Canal Zone in Panama, and the broad intent of the Monroe Doctrine. It appeared that the President's "Big Stick" policy was indeed a roaring success.

The election campaign of 1904 was practically a formality. He ultimately won by a landslide. Nevertheless, he worried about the outcome throughout the campaign. When the returns came in on election night, he was thunderstruck with emotion. "I am stunned by the overwhelming victory we have won. I had no conception that such a thing was possible. I had thought it probable we should win, but was quite prepared to be defeated. But of course, I had not the slightest idea that there was such a tidal wave of support." [87] He quipped to Edith, "My dear, I am no longer a political accident." [88]

During his second administration his popularity only soared to greater and greater heights. Unfortunately for him, that did not necessarily translate into legislative success. Much of his policy agenda was ignored by a lackadaisical Congress–not so much out of substantive opposition, as out of indolent satisfaction with the status quo. As a result, he grew more and more restless as the months and years passed.

Perhaps that is why he stuck to his guns about not running for a third term. There was no constitutional provision to prevent it–and there was little doubt that he would be easily re-elected if he chose that course. He maintained his self-imposed lame duck status nevertheless.

Apart from the construction of the Panama Canal, a determined fight against segregated schools, and the dramatic strengthening of the National Parks and Forests system, his final months in office were essentially ceremonial. Perhaps his most significant achievement in those final days was the selection of his successor. And in that he had made a dastardly error–or so he later thought.

He designated his secretary of war as his heir apparent. A 350-pound former Ohio Supreme Court judge, William Howard Taft hardly cut the same heroic figure as Roosevelt. But all he needed to gain the nomination and win the election was a nod from the president. And that he got.

Though the nation cried out for "four more years," Roosevelt was resolute.[89] During the Republican Convention, delegates pledged to Taft staged an hour-long demonstration in an attempt to somehow convince the president to change his mind. Even after Taft's nomination, spontaneous rallies on behalf of Roosevelt cropped up across the nation. In the end though, he insured that his dour and corpulent friend would indeed succeed him. Taft was elected, though–everyone agreed–only as the proxy of the great man who had preceded him.

On March 4, 1909, Theodore Roosevelt and his family left the White House with a round of bittersweet farewells.

A RESTLESS HEART

I do not number party loyalty among my commandments.[90]

*I*mmediately after leaving office, Roosevelt left the country for a year-long safari in Africa, followed by a grand tour of Europe with his family. The trip included hunting, reading, conducting scientific experiments, hiking, and swimming. In short, he did all the things he so dearly loved to do–the things that the press of public responsibility had prevented him from doing over the past several years.

But he had an ulterior motive for his long absence. "My main reason for wishing to go to Africa for a year," he confided to friends, "is so I can get where no one can accuse me of running, nor do Taft the injustice of accusing him of permitting me to run the job." [91] He wanted to give Taft a chance to make his own way.

Alas, it quickly became apparent that Taft had instead lost his way.

From weeks-old newspapers and letters from friends, Roosevelt learned his successor was bungling the job–and that already he was on the verge of tearing asunder the successful Republican coalition Roosevelt had worked so hard to pull together.

Taft had cast a languid sleepy spell over the government in Washington–yielding to the whims and wiles of Wall Street industrialists and big city machine bosses. It was not a happy contrast with the man who had preceded him in office. Taft was a decent man; there was no disputing that. But he seemed to lack vision. Though he had a brilliant legal mind and vast foreign policy experience, he appeared bland and inarticulate. He seemed to have no ideas of his own–and even those he did have seemed muddled. By all appearances, he epitomized an entrenched and institutional politics-as-usual. He had unwittingly allowed the White House to become captive to powerful vested interests. He was a follower, not a leader.

Meanwhile, Roosevelt was wrapping up his successful safari with a round of visits with the sundry kings, emperors, presidents, and prelates of Europe. At Cambridge, where he delivered a major scientific paper, he was introduced as "The peer of the most august kings, queller of wars, destroyer of monsters wherever found, yet the most human of mankind, before whose coming comets took to flight, and all the startled mouths of seven-fold Nile took flight." [92] Thus, the contrast between the two men was only heightened. Dissatisfaction with Taft became pandemic.

Life magazine heralded the return of Roosevelt to America:

> *Teddy, come home and blow your horn,*
> *The sheep's in the meadow, the cow's in the corn.*
> *The boy you left to tend and keep,*
> *Is under the haystack fast asleep.*[93]

Although he attempted to avoid commenting publicly on the domestic strife now brewing in Washington, privately he began to express genuine concern that Taft might undo all the good he had accomplished during the previous administrations. When he arrived in New York on June 18, 1910, the pressure to jump into the fray became almost irresistible.

Whistles shrieked, horns blew, salutes were fired, and the largest crowd ever gathered in one place on American soil greeted Roosevelt's return. He was at the zenith of his popularity. It was a brilliant, sunny day.

But the storm clouds were gathering.

Gradually, in the next several weeks and months, the contrast between Roosevelt and Taft was transformed into a genuine conflict of ideals. Eventually, Roosevelt felt he had to speak out and oppose the direction in which his old friend had chosen to lead the nation.

That was a fateful decision. According to Henry Cabot Lodge, "That one decision may well have altered the course of our nation's history—indeed the history of the whole world—more than any other single decision in the course of the last fifty years." [94]

Indeed, it may well have.

1912

My hat is in the ring.[95]

O
f all his adventures and accomplishments, Roosevelt's involvement in the presidential race of 1912 was perhaps his most significant–and certainly, his most controversial. That year, the electorate was confounded by a whole host of dire dilemmas. The lackluster Taft administration had created a real conundrum for voters.

The fiery Democratic nominee was Woodrow Wilson. Though he had served briefly–and without notable distinction–as governor of New Jersey, he was essentially a political unknown. And yet, because the campaign hinged on the issue of change, anything seemed possible.

According to Wilson, change was essential. "Our life has broken away from the past," he said.[96] "Old political formulas do not fit the present problems."[97] He believed that: "This is nothing short of a new social age, a new era of human relationships, a new stage setting for the drama of life."[98] He was convinced that the "new age" demanded "new circumstances" and the "fitting of a new social organization."[99] He wanted to "bring the government back to the people" through an aggressive implementation of activist legislation, adjudication, and administration.[100] He advocated radical change: "Politics in America is a case which sadly requires attention. The system set up by our law and our usage doesn't work–or at least it cannot be depended on." [101]

He boasted that Americans had an obligation to reinvent the world by "interpreting the Constitution according to the Darwinian principle" and by becoming "architects in our time." [102] He foresaw the advent of "a glorious New World Order" and "a marvelous New Freedom." [103]

Because Taft seemed either unwilling or unable to deflect Wilson's energetic barrage of ideological rhetoric, Theodore Roosevelt reluctantly came out of retirement and took to the stump. He decried the liberalism of Wilson saying that the nation should be "ruled by the Ten Commandments" not "by Darwinian presumption." [104] He claimed that "the great heart of the nation beats for truth, honor, and liberty," and thus he felt compelled to decry "the immorality and absurdity" of Wilson's "doctrines of socialism." [105] He asserted that he was an "old school conservative" who believed in "the progressive notions" that made for "a strong people and a tame government." [106]

Taft was chagrined. He fought back with a derisive negative campaign. He accused his old friend Roosevelt of "reckless ambition." [107] He chided his old boss of "unsettling of the fundamentals of our government" and called him a "serious menace and an extremist." [108]

Roosevelt handily won the hearts of the grassroots and secured nine out of every ten electable delegates sent to the national convention. However, he was eventually denied the Republican nomination through a series of last-minute back room maneuvers by key members of the party establishment–

who were afraid they would not be able to control the always independent-minded Roosevelt.

Scandalized and demoralized, the Republicans divided–the "moderates" stood by Taft while the "progressives" remained loyal to Roosevelt. The fractious campaign would be a three-way race–with the popular Roosevelt leading a fledgling third-party effort.

The politics-as-usual finagling, mudslinging, and conniving outraged the popular press and exacerbated the electorate. Disaffection with the entire process ran rampant. Roosevelt angrily charged:

> *The old parties are husks, with no real soul*
> *within either, divided on artificial lines, boss*
> *ridden and privilege controlled, each a jumble*
> *of incongruous elements and neither daring to*
> *speak out wisely and fearlessly what should be*
> *said on the vital issues of the day.*[109]

As the campaign progressed, it appeared that his last-minute third party challenge might actually defy all odds and succeed. Though he had virtually no money, no organization, and no political apparatus behind him, his sheer popularity and force of will threatened to carry the day.

But then, with less than three weeks to go, Roosevelt was the victim of an assassination attempt. Though his wound was not mortal, he was unable to return to the rigors of the campaign. Uncertainty suddenly gripped the electorate. Torn between the two old familiar parties and the one national leader they could trust, voters were frozen in indecision. They stayed away in droves.

On election day, ambivalence reigned. None of the candidates received a majority. Though Wilson attained a weak plurality against Roosevelt, and was thus declared the winner, nearly sixty percent of the popular vote had actually gone against him. As a result, he entered the White House the next year without any semblance of a mandate, facing a formidable array of opposition forces.

Roosevelt, on the other hand, though somewhat discouraged by the outcome, took solace in the fact that he had overcome all the odds; with little more than public affection on his side–he was outspent by each of his opponents by more than ten-to-one–he had very nearly toppled the supremacy of the two establishment parties.

He was still only fifty-four years old. Nevertheless, he felt certain that he had heard his "last hurrah" in the rough and tumble world of politics.[110]

YEARS OF EXILE

Better faithful than famous. [111]

"*I* have to go. It is my last chance to be a boy." [112] With those words Roosevelt launched the most dangerous wilderness expedition of his long and remarkable career as an outdoorsman. Finding the radical posturing and preening of the Wilson administration difficult to face, he had arranged to join an expedition to map the unexplored River of Doubt, which flowed though the heart of Brazil's dense Amazonian rain forest.

It was to be a dangerous and harrowing expedition–fighting off everything from fierce fire ants and giant red wasps to aggressive piranhas and poisonous reptiles. The explorers disappeared into the dense wilderness for more than two months. During the journey, two men were lost as well as five of their seven canoes, and most of their supplies and provisions. Most members of the expedition contracted dysentery and malaria–including Roosevelt and his son Kermit.

When the party at last emerged from the jungle, having successfully mapped the 1,500 mile-long river, they discovered that they had been given up for dead. Roosevelt had lost 57 pounds and severely injured his leg. He would never fully recover. He returned to a world that was about to engage in a war from which it would never fully recover either.

As the regional Balkan hostilities began to escalate into the First World War during the summer of 1914, Roosevelt was transformed into a kind of prophet in the wilderness. He believed Americans would ultimately be drawn into the war and ought to therefore prepare themselves against that day. Once again his instincts were startlingly accurate. But this time, his was an unwelcome message. Americans were in an isolationist mood–and they believed, against all evidence to the contrary, that preparedness might actually draw them into the widening conflict. Though he was personally as popular as ever, the public, on the whole, refused to heed Roosevelt's dire warnings–until it was too late.

He wrote books, made speeches, lobbied his old allies in Washington. But he was branded a war-monger, an extremist, an alarmist. Like Winston Churchill would be in the years prior to the Second World War, Roosevelt was vilified by iso-lationists and accommodationists alike. But he never wavered in his convictions, and his voice refused to be drowned out by the din of public opinion.

When at last his prediction of American involvement in the war was fulfilled, each of his four sons, as well as one son-in-law, immediately volunteered. Roosevelt himself sought to raise and lead a division into battle–just as he had during the Spanish-American War. But President Wilson would hear none of it–that was the last thing the beleaguered President needed: Theodore Roosevelt leading a heroic charge across the battlefields of Belgium and France.

Feeling somewhat vindicated by the turn of events, Roosevelt led the war effort at home. He helped the sale of

bonds. He made speeches to raise morale. He lobbied for better provisioning. His star seemed, at last, on the ascendancy
again. Americans began to look upon their old hero for a
sense of direction in such disconcerting times. The Republican
Party even began to entertain the idea of putting his name
forward to lead their ticket in 1920.

But then on July 16, 1918, Roosevelt learned his youngest
son had been killed in a aerial dogfight over German lines.
His stoic exterior belied the devastation he and Edith felt.
Issuing a public statement he said, "Quentin's mother and I
are very glad that he got to the front and had a chance to ren-
der some service to his country, and to show the stuff that was
in him before his fate befell him." [113] Later he would assert,
"Only those are fit to live who do not fear to die; and none
are fit to die who have shrunk from the joy of life and the
duty of life." [114]

In truth, the death somehow broke his heretofore
indomitable spirit. During the next six months, the nagging
effects of his malaria and recurring bouts of inflammatory
rheumatism and gout would hobble him time and again.
Though he remained as busy as ever standing for the cause
of reform–prompting Republican leaders to continue to pro-
mote him for the 1920 ticket–he was obviously suffering a
serious physical decline. At long last, it appeared that he had
worn out his body. He was in and out of the hospital several
times during the winter.

The doctors let him go home for Christmas–but with a
warning. They threatened that he might well be confined to a
wheelchair for the rest of his life if he didn't slow down. Of
course he had no intention whatsoever of slowing down. He
retorted crisply, "All right then. I can work that way, too." [115]

Two weeks later, on January 5, 1919, he worked on several articles before retiring fitfully to bed. Before drifting off

to sleep he told Edith, "I wonder if you will ever know how much I love Sagamore Hill." [116] At about four o'clock the next morning, an old friend staying at the house became alarmed at Roosevelt's irregular breathing. He called for a nurse, but before anyone could arrive Roosevelt had stopped breathing. Edith was awakened and rushed to her husband's side. "Theodore, darling," she called to him softly. "Theodore, darling." [117] But there was no reply.

"The old lion is dead," [118] was all the cable read that was sent later that morning.

VINDICATION

*Weasel words from mollycoddles will never do when
the day demands prophetic clarity from greathearts.*[119]

The funeral of Theodore Roosevelt was a quiet family
affair at Oyster Bay within sight of his beloved
Sagamore Hill home. It was there, accompanied by the
hushed strains of his favorite hymn, George Keith's *How Firm
a Foundation*, that he was laid to rest.

But America–indeed the world–would not be content
with such a private end to such a public life.

Hundreds, perhaps even thousands, of memorial services
were held across the land. Messages of grief, sorrow, and con-
dolence poured in from around the globe–from kings and
princes to paupers and pedestrians. Accolades, eulogies, trib-
utes, and reminiscences were published, broadcast, and
announced at every turn. It seemed everyone, from the
mighty to the obscure, desired to have their say about the
great man.

On February 9, 1919, a memorial service was held in
Congress–and afterwards a reverent prayer vigil was held.

Henry Cabot Lodge, his dearest friend, closest confidant, and political mentor, spoke in halting tones of a man like no other man any of them had ever known:

> *He had a touch of the knight errant in his daily life, although he would have never admitted it; but it was there. It was not visible in the medieval form of shining armor and dazzling tournaments but in the never-ceasing effort to help the poor and oppressed, to defend and protect women and children, to right the wronged and succor the downtrodden. Passing by on the other side was not a mode of travel through life ever possible to him; and yet he was as far distant from the professional philanthropist or the liberal do-gooder as could well be imagined, for all he tried to do to help his fellow men he regarded as a part of the day's work to be done and not talked about. No man ever prized sentiment or hated sentimentality more than he. He preached unceasingly the familiar morals which lie at the bottom of both family and public life. The blood of some ancestral Scotch Covenanter or of some Dutch Reformed preacher facing down tyranny was in his veins, and with his large opportunities and vast audiences he was always ready to appeal for justice and righteousness. But his own particular ideals he never attempted to thrust upon the world until the day came when they were to be translated into realities of personal action.*[120]

He concluded, saying:

> *Indeed, the absolute purity and integrity of his*
> *family life–where those ideals first met the test*
> *of authenticity–tell us why the pride and inter-*
> *est which his fellow countrymen felt in him*
> *were always touched with the warm light of*
> *love. In the home so dear to him, in his sleep,*
> *death came, and. . .so, Valiant-for-Truth passed*
> *over and all the trumpets sounded for him on*
> *the other side.*[121]

Whether poet, bard, jester, or knave, it seemed the world's testimony of him was but one:

> *He dwelt with the tribes of the marsh and moor,*
> *He sat at the board of kings;*
> *He tasted the toil of the burdened slave*
> *And the joy that triumph brings.*
> *But whether to jungle or palace hall*
> *Or white-walled tent he came,*
> *He was brother to king and soldier and slave,*
> *His welcome was the same.*[122]

But of all the things said about him in the days and weeks following his sudden death, the greatest tribute to Theodore Roosevelt's legacy of service came from the political arena–as he would have wished.

Woodrow Wilson proved to be a supremely unpopular president. He acted decisively to implement his radical agenda–four constitutional amendments were passed that revolutionized the nature of American governance–and he was able to concentrate vast new powers in the hands of the central government. However, Wilson was never able to win popular support. Though he had somehow survived a tepid reelection bid, virtually all of his proposals and policies were met with ignominious defeat. Even his proposals for the cessation of hostilities following the First World War, his famed Fourteen Points and the League of Nations, were repudiated at home.

By the end of Wilson's second term, the whole conception of activist government had been thoroughly repudiated. The President was mired in scandalous unpopularity. His administration was a disaster. The world was in shambles following the war. And the peace of Versailles portended even worse. Democracy had done all that Socialism had threatened to do.

The electorate realized that it must rally from its dismal and equivocal mindset. And so it did.

Warren G. Harding, the conservative Republican candidate, issued a clarion call for a return to "normalcy." He said:

> *America's present need is not heroics, but healing; not nostrums, but normalcy; not revolution, but restoration; not agitation, but adjustment; not surgery, but serenity. The world needs to be reminded that all human ills are not curable by legislation, and that quantity of statutory enactment and excess of government offer no substitute for quality of citizenship.*[123]

America was ready for a return to the quiet certainty that while politics is important, it is not all-important. Voters had to abandon their natural reticence and ambivalence. They realized that sometimes political involvement must take precedence in our lives in order to insure that political involvement does not take preeminence over our lives. They had learned that lesson the hard way.

They gave Harding a landslide victory. Ultimately though, it was a victory for Roosevelt–the platform the Republicans ran on was virtually identical to the one he had espoused just a few years prior. Harding ran self-consciously as a "Roosevelt Republican." [124]

Even as his image was being carved into the face of Mount Rushmore–joining the pantheon of America's greatest men–the impress of his leadership was again looming large over the land.

"He being dead, yet speaketh." [125]

PART II:
THE CHARACTER OF THEODORE ROOSEVELT

"It is not the critic that counts; not the man who points out how the strong man stumbles, or where the doer of deeds could have done better. The credit belongs to the man who is actually in the arena, whose face is marred by dust and sweat and blood; who strives valiantly, who errs, and comes short again and again, because there is no effort without error and shortcoming; but who does actually strive to do the deeds." [126]

HIS FAMILY

I have had the happiest home life of any man I have ever known.[127]

*T*heodore Roosevelt found his greatest joy not in power, fame, wealth, or even adventure, but in his family. There is much about his life and career that may be open to dispute, but on this issue there can be little doubt. According to his own testimony, it was his family that was the source of his strength, the locus of his vocation, and the well-spring of his values:

> *No other success in life–not being President, or being wealthy, or going to college, or anything else–comes up to the success of the man and woman who can feel that they have done their duty and that their children and grandchildren rise up to call them blesse.*[128]

At a time when the Victorian family ethic was still very much in vogue–positing that children should be seen and not

heard and that domesticity was a singularly feminine concern–Roosevelt was notable for his dissent. He loved his home
life–and all that attended it.

He was a hopeless romantic who wrote affectionate letters to Edith on an almost daily basis. He regularly sent her
flowers, adorned her with jewelry, and made certain that they
had time alone together–regardless of his hectic schedule. She
was his best friend, his confidante, and his lover. He fully
believed that, "The greatest privilege, the greatest duty for any
man is to be happily married." [129] And he was.

But it was his relationship with his children that best
demonstrates the priority he placed on family life. Visitors to
Sagamore Hill or the White House always were amazed by
both the exuberance and the predominance of the great man's
participation in "childish things." [130] He often postponed
important affairs of state to play with the children. He taught
them to swim and hunt and row and sail and ride. He often
took them on what he dubbed his "rambles and romps"
through the woods–a rigorous bee-line hike that made no
compensation for hills, fences, streams, or undergrowth.

Once the Japanese ambassador was surprised to discover
the president on his hands and knees roaring down the hall-
way outside the Oval Office chasing a gaggle of squealing
children–a real live Teddy Bear. A distinguished British guest
staying in the Lincoln bedroom was awakened late one night
by a rambunctious game of touch football up and down the
White House corridor. Right in the middle of the ruckus was,
much to his dismay, the Leader of the Free World.

Roosevelt allowed the White House to be turned into a
regular menagerie of strange pets. At various times the children enjoyed the presence of a lion, a hyena, a coyote, several
bears, an owl, kangaroo rats, flying squirrels, rabbits, and
guinea pigs. And of course, the White House stables featured

a goodly variety of ponies, donkeys, thoroughbreds, and even a zebra. It was a child's paradise.

All four of his boys idolized him. Both of his daughters believed him to be their knight in shining armor. His oldest child, Alice, once asserted that he was "a King Arthur, a William Wallace, and a Buffalo Bill all rolled into one." [131] When his youngest son, Quinten, was asked by a White House journalist to describe the president in a single word, he quickly responded. "Fun," he said. "Papa is fun." [132]

Of course, Roosevelt was not all fun and games. He was a strict disciplinarian who tolerated many things–but disrespect, disobedience, and discourtesy were not among them. He took it upon himself to be the enforcer of the family standards–he filled their lives with good books, great ideas, marvelous adventures, and open affections. He taught them the Catechism and conducted family devotions–albeit sporadically–from the time they were very small.

He believed that private life was the proving ground for public life. "A man must do well in his own home," he argued, "before he can do well outside." [133] To be certain, he practiced what he preached.

As they grew into adulthood, he became for his children a beloved intimate. His letters to them were published as paragons of the ideal family. Not surprisingly, each child carried the standard of his father's faith and ideals throughout their lives. It would be difficult–indeed, altogether impossible–to comprehend all that he was and all that he did apart from this unshakable commitment to his family. For Theodore Roosevelt, family values were the essential foundation stones for all other values:

> *There is need to develop all the virtues that*
> *have the state for their sphere of action; but*

*these virtues are as dust in a windy street
unless back of them lie the strong and tender
virtues of a family life based upon the love of
the one man for the one woman and on their
joyous and fearless acceptance of their common
obligation to the children that are theirs.*[134]

HIS FATHER

My father was the best man I ever knew. He combined strength and courage with gentleness, tenderness, and great unselfishness.[135]

Theodore Roosevelt came by his family values honestly–he gained them from his family, and in particular, his father. The way the great man deported himself in public and private–from the time he was a youngster to the time he was the best-known and best-loved man in America–was a determined effort to simply follow in the footsteps of his father.

Though he died when he was only 46, Roosevelt's father was a man of extraordinary character and accomplishment. A successful businessman, a tireless philanthropist, a determined patriot, a committed family man, a refined intellectual, a faithful Christian, and an energetic outdoorsman, he was everything that Roosevelt himself always strove to be.

According to the journalist Jacob Riis, he was "a man of untiring energy, of prodigious industry, the most valiant fighter in his day for the right, and the winner of his fights."[136] Not surprisingly, his son would often sigh when, as governor or colonel or president, he had accomplished something for which his father had striven and paved the way, "Oh, how I wish Father were here and could see it." [137]

It was from his father that Roosevelt gained his great love of life: "He drove a four-in-hand in the park, sailed a boat, loved the woods, shared in every athletic sport, and was the life of every company," [138] he remembered. But it was also from his father that he developed a sense of justice, righteousness, and discipline:

> *He would not tolerate in us children selfishness, cruelty, idleness, cowardice, or untruthfulness. With great love and patience and the most understanding and consideration, he combined insistence on discipline. He never physically punished me but once, but he was the only man of whom I was ever really afraid. I do not mean that it was a wrong fear, for he was entirely just, and we children adored him.* [139]

Roosevelt was convinced that leadership could not exist in isolation. Leadership had to be modeled after some tangible, practical, and realizable ideal. Thus, all great leaders were, in truth, simply students of men of unimpeachable character, unreproachable courage, and unswerving vision. Leaders had mentors. They were disciples. Rather than striking out as lonely pioneers, they were willing to stand on the shoulders of those who had gone before. They were men who comprehended the sober notion of legacy.

Thus, he never attempted to escape from the shadow of his father. He never tried to establish an independent reputation for himself. Instead, he always felt that he was accountable to a kind of family trust and a national covenant. In his mind, he was essentially an heir, not a progenitor:

> *We have been entrusted with much–each and every one of us. We have a glorious inheritance that we must honor. I have a special sense of that great legacy, being the son of the finest man, the happiest man, I have ever known. He showed me what it means to live for right. He was a living illustration of the American ideal and spirit. All that I have ever done has been little more than an attempt to live up to and honor that legacy.*[140]

Undoubtedly, it was this sense of legacy that animated Roosevelt's commitment to his own children and grandchildren. He wanted to make certain that all the benefits he had enjoyed–the special bequest of his father's legacy–would be enjoyed by them as well. He was conscious of the fact that a great responsibility of every generation of parents is not so much to exercise leadership, but to pass on to their children the necessary principles and resources for leadership–and then leave the outcome to providence.

Jacob Riis believed that the son was "intent on making his life but a monument to the father."[141] But because of that "selfless obedience," his life instead "became, in the hands of God's good providence, a monument to the hopes and dreams of us all."[142]

Of such uncommon character is true leadership forged.

THE STRENUOUS LIFE

I am of course in a perfect whirl of work and have
every kind of worry and trouble–but that's what I am
here for, and down at bottom, I enjoy it after all.[143]

*R*oosevelt's passion for life was infectious. Everything about him tingled with zest and vitality. He approached every circumstance and situation with consummate gusto and enthusiasm. What others believed were obstacles, he considered adventures. What others thought of as setbacks, he viewed as challenges.

As a result, children loved him–he had a flair for the dramatic and the heroic. And he lived in perpetual motion. Adults were often struck utterly speechless in his presence–his energies were often incomprehensible, and always irrepressible.

When he was president, he took visiting dignitaries on his point-to-point "rambles and romps" through Rock Creek Park. Setting a blistering pace, he would cut a bee-line course climbing over, wading through, cutting under, or swimming across whatever crossed his path. Washington observers were always amused by the sight of the great man charging ahead while his guests desperately struggled to keep up.

Once while hiking and climbing in the Adirondacks, he had a Secret Service agent lower him with a rope around his ankles into a wide gorge, so he could take a close-up photograph of a bird's nest. But when the agent tried to pull the president up the cliff, he was unable to manage. Impatient, Roosevelt called to the man, "Just cut the rope." Horrified, the agent refused—there was a thirty-foot drop between the president and the rushing water below. "Cut the rope," Roosevelt insisted. By this time the agent was panic stricken—but he could think of nothing to do. At last, the president took matters into his own hands and cut the rope himself. He plunged into the icy waters below. Terrified, the agent scrambled down a trail to the bottom of the gorge to discover the president lying at the water's edge, half-conscious, cut, bruised, and soaked to the bone. The great man looked up at him, smiled a huge toothy grin, and said, "My, wasn't that just bully!"

Roosevelt had a boxing ring set up in the White House and often invited professional prizefighters to go a few rounds with him. He was an avid football fan—and eventually helped to establish the National Collegiate Athletic Association so that the sport could be regulated. And of course, he went hunting and fishing every chance he could get.

And it was not only his pursuit of daring physical activity that astonished his more placid contemporaries—he seemed to work more, read more, think more, study more, talk more and do more than any other living man. People simply could not believe how diverse were his interests and his accomplishments. Henry Cabot Lodge called him "a living tornado." [144] Henry Adams said he "crams more into a day than most men can hope to in a month." [145] And John Hay quipped, "I get tired just thinking about his schedule." [146]

In short, Theodore Roosevelt indulged in an unprecedented life of unceasing activity. And yet his intense ardor was not the result of mere hyperactivity. It was the carefully worked out result of his credo. It was the manifestation of his worldview. It was the essence of his philosophy of life:

> *I wish to preach not the doctrine of ignoble*
> *ease but the doctrine of the strenuous life; the*
> *life of toil and effort; of labor and strife; to*
> *preach that highest form of success which*
> *comes not to the man who desires mere easy*
> *peace but to the man who does not shrink from*
> *danger, hardship, or from the bitter toil, and*
> *who out of these wins the splendid ultimate*
> *triumph.* [147]

Roosevelt did not believe greatness could be inherited. Our great legacy merely affords us with potential. It is up to each succeeding generation to give a good account of what they have been given. "Leaders are those," he asserted, "who make the most of every moment, of every opportunity, and of every available resource." [148]

To be sure, he practiced what he preached.

THE GREAT OUTDOORS

*I love all the seasons: the snows and bare woods of
winter, the rush of growing things and the blossom
spray of spring, the leafy shades that are heralded by
the green dance of summer, and the sharp fall winds
that tear the brilliant banners with which the trees
greet the dying year.*[149]

*T*heodore Roosevelt loved the mystery, the beauty, and
the majesty of creation. Almost every aspect of his
life–from the way he raised his children to the way he conducted his politics, from the way he spent his leisure time to
the way the way he pursued his intellectual interests, from the
way he related to other men to the way he invested his
resources–revolved around his passion for the natural world.

He spent almost every minute he could outdoors. His
enthusiastic involvement in hiking through the woods, riding
horseback across the fields, hunting in the wilderness, rowing
across lakes and bays–to say nothing of his climbing, sailing,
swimming, trekking, picnicking, bird-watching, and garden-
ing–was legendary. He was by all accounts "the greatest
sportsman of his day." [150]

All of Roosevelt's most beautiful and eloquent writing–the foreword to *African Game Trails, A Booklover's Holidays in the Open,* and *The Wilderness Hunter*–vibrate to this note of a passionate love of nature. His letters are filled with observations from nature. His speeches make generous use of outdoor allusions and illustrations. His mind was utterly possessed by the glory of the created order.

John Burroughs, the great naturalist, declared that he did not know "any man with a keener and more comprehensive interest in nature and wild life–an interest both scientific and human." [151] Indeed, very few could even come close to matching his field skills, knowledge, or instincts.

Once, while visiting Yellowstone National Park, he thought he had heard the rather indistinct song of a Bullock's Oriole. The scientists and naturalists accompanying the president assured him that he must be mistaken. Though such birds were known in the area, it was much too early–by a matter of months–for them to make an appearance. "Well, I am nearly certain that I caught a hint of two brief notes which could not be those of any other," he replied. Gently, the experts attempted to disabuse Roosevelt of the obviously mistaken notion. "Perhaps you have the song twisted," they suggested. But then, that evening as they were concluding their meal, the president suddenly laid down his fork, exclaiming, "Look! Look!" On a shrub outside the cabin window was a Bullock's Oriole. The men were astonished. Roosevelt simply grinned and said, "Aha. Just as I suspected." [152]

One of the practical ends of his love of creation was the launching of a viable movement to protect and conserve America's natural resources. According to the *Encyclopedia Britannica,* "If Roosevelt did not invent the term conservation, he literally created as well as led the movement which made conservation one of the foremost political and social questions in the United States." [153] Certainly, the priority he placed on setting apart the great remaining wilderness areas, nature preserves, and wooded lands to be held in perpetuity as National Parks and Forests was one of the chief accomplishments of his administration. He believed it was incumbent upon every generation to ensure that the succeeding generations would have the same opportunities to appreciate, enjoy, and benefit from the splendor of the nation's natural resources.

Even so, he would hardly have sympathized with modern environmentalism. As Edward Wagenknecht has argued, "He never sentimentalized nature or denied that it was red in tooth and claw." [154] His love of nature did not obscure his comprehension of its fallen estate and its ultimate subservience to the interests of man.

Leadership is the art of pursuing the ideal in the midst of a world that is less than ideal–and never losing sight of either notion. Thus, the stewardship of nature was Roosevelt's chief concern, not the sanctity of nature. Such balance is rare indeed.

AN APPETITE FOR LEARNING

I am rather more apt to read old books than new ones.[155]

*F*rancis Bacon once mused, "Histories make men wise; poets, witty; mathematics, subtle; natural philosophy, deep; morals, grave; logic and rhetoric, able to contend."[156] Theodore Roosevelt took that counsel to heart. He was a voracious learner and an avid reader throughout his extraordinary life.

Among his friends he counted the greatest writers, thinker, scholars, and scientists of his day. And by all accounts he was the best read of them all–being readily conversant on everything from the traditional classics to the most recent philosophical, sociological, or technological musings. He usually read at least five books a week–unless he wasn't too busy, in which case he read more. And yet his attitude toward the torrid pace of his intellectual pursuit was refreshingly relaxed:

> *I am old-fashioned, or sentimental, or something about books. Whenever I read one I want,*

in the first place, to enjoy myself, and, in the
next place, to feel that I am a little better and
not a little worse for having read it.[157]

His son Quentin claimed that his father read every book received at the Library of Congress–which of course he did not. But many of his friends testified that however new the volume they recommended to him, he had always read it already. "His range of reading is amazing," wrote the brilliant writer H.G. Wells. "He seems to be echoing with all the thought of the time, and he has receptivity to the pitch of genius." [158] Guglielmo Marconi, the great Italian physicist and inventor, was amazed by his knowledge in the specialized field of Italian history and literature. "That man actually cited book after book that I've never heard of, much less read. He's going to keep me busy for some time just following his Italian reading." [159] English diplomat Lord Charnwood asserted, "No statesman for centuries has had his width of intellectual range." [160]

As a result of his relentless studies and his near perfect recall, his knowledge was highly integrated, and he was continually crossing boundaries, moving back and forth from one area of human knowledge to another. He was thus able to make connections that mere specialists were unable to make.

According to Viscount Lee, "Whether the subject of the moment was political economy, the Greek drama, tropical fauna or flora, the Irish sagas, protective coloration in nature, metaphysics, the technique of football, or post-futurist painting, he was equally at home with the experts and drew out the best that was in them." [161] Indeed, "In one afternoon," said his son Archie, "I have heard him speak to the foremost Bible student of the world, a prominent ornithologist, an Asian diplomat, and a French general, all of whom agreed that

Father knew more about the subjects in which they had specialized than they did."

Indeed, his mind was omnivorous and his interests were dizzying. "Can you come for dinner either Wednesday or Friday?" he wrote to Henry Cabot Lodge's wife. "Then we could discuss the Hittite Empire, the Pithecanthropus, Magyar love songs, the exact relations of the Atli of the *Volsunga Saga* to the Etzel of the *Nibelungenlied,* and both to Attila–with interludes about the rate bill, Beveridge, and other matters of more vivid contemporary interest."

But for all his prodigious knowledge, he was supremely unpretentious. All he ever claimed for himself was zest, "delight in the play of the mind for its own sake." [162] But others were rather more impressed. The famed academic, Vilhjalmur Stefansson asserted, "It is to be supposed, seeing that Roosevelt is human, that there must be some fields in which he is ill-informed, but none of these have ever come to my attention, nor, so far as I know, to the attention of any of my friends in the various spheres of scientific or cultural exploration." [163]

"If you want to lead, you must read," was a maxim that Roosevelt took seriously. [164] It was merely an extension of his philosophy of life: making the most of his mind was of a piece with making the most of his body. It was merely an exercise of good stewardship.

And exercise it, he did.

STORY-TELLER

I am in the mood for a good story. Of course, I am always in the mood for a good story.[165]

*R*oosevelt had all the gifts and inclinations of a born story-teller. Not only did he have a vivid imagination, an insatiable curiosity, a rich classical education, a profound grasp of history, and an elephantine memory, he loved sharing his many enthusiasms with others. He loved to talk. And his gregarious personality seemed to naturally animate whatever he talked about.

Of all that he accomplished throughout the crowded hours of his life, story-telling was among his favorite occupations. In fact, he wove story-telling into all of his other activities as best he could. His speeches were filled with vignettes from history. His conversations regularly recounted heroic incidents and episodes from the past. His correspondence was well seasoned with the lessons of yore. His favorite time of day was when he would gather his children around him for a bed-time story each evening. For years he taught a boys' Sunday School class–primarily because he so loved telling and retelling the stories of the Bible.

His friends testified that he was a dominating conversationalist–and that could be rather intimidating at times. He was always more than a little rambunctious, especially when he became enthralled with the course of a discussion–he was an incorrigible table thumper, conversation interrupter, and backslapper. Richard Watson Gilder said he was "a human volcano, roaring as only a human volcano can roar–leading the laughing and the singing and the shouting, like a boy out of school, pounding the table with both noisy fists." [166] Gamaliel Bradford quipped that, "He killed mosquitoes as if they were lions and lions as if they were mosquitoes." [167] Everyone around him was either utterly captivated and enthralled or entirely exhausted and cowed. But either way, they all agreed, he had a knack for rich and compelling prose–often pouring forth in an unending stream.

Of course, his story-telling prowess was not limited to his speeches, monologues, and conversations. From his earliest youth to full maturity, Roosevelt wrote furiously on everything that interested him. Indeed, there were long stretches of his life when writing provided his principal income.

According to Mark Twain, if Theodore Roosevelt had not gone into politics, "he might have completely dominated America's literary scene." [168] Robert Frost asserted that Roosevelt had the "innate ability to craft sterling prose and gripping narrative." [169] Julian Street said that "Roosevelt was a congenital writer and story-teller." [170] And Henry Cabot Lodge claimed that Roosevelt possessed "a rare and instinctive grasp of the art of narrative prose–he could have excelled as a journalist, an historian, a novelist, or a playwright." [171] As it was, Roosevelt somehow wrote almost sixty books during his mind-bogglingly busy career–books of stunning variety–ranging from biographies and histories to natural science and current political controversy.

Several of the books are acknowledged classics in their fields. *The Naval War of 1812*–which was hardly more than the work of a boy–remains a required text at naval academies on both sides of the Atlantic. *The Winning of the West* is placed alongside the histories of Francis Parkman as among the best of its kind. *Hunting Trips of a Ranchman, Ranch Life and the Hunting Trail,* and *The Wilderness Hunter* created an entirely new genre and spawned interest in the "wild, wild West." His profiles of *Thomas Hart Benton, Gouverneur Morris,* and *Oliver Cromwell* continue to serve as correctives to the smothering dominance of academic scientism in modern historical and biographical studies. And his controversial tomes, *Realizable Goals, Fear God and Take Your Own Part,* and *The Foes of Our Own Household* ring more prophetically true today than even in his own day.

Despite his great prolificacy and his obvious inclinations toward the story-telling art, Roosevelt never took his gift for granted. Nor did he find the task of committing his thoughts to words carefree and effortless:

> *Writing is horribly hard work to me; and I*
> *make slow progress. My style is very rough and*
> *I do not like a certain lack of sequitur that I do*
> *not seem to be able to get out of it.*[172]

Nevertheless, he saw the proclamation of his essential principles as a vital aspect of his calling. He did not believe that he could lead the nation if he could not vividly portray the path down which he wished to take it. Indeed, "Where there is no vision, the people perish." [173] And so, until he took his final breath, he was a compelling and compulsive story-teller.

GOOD DEEDS

I have a horror of words that are not translated into deeds, of speech that does not result in action[174]

According to Shakespeare, "Talkers are generally no good doers."[175] But there can be little doubt that Theodore Roosevelt violated that rule; though a talker, he was also a remarkable good doer.

The offices he held, the movements he led, the reforms he insured, the feats he achieved, and the accomplishments that he attained seemed to have been enough for a dozen lifetimes. But for him, there were always new vistas, new hazards, and new demands that drove him onward.

Perhaps the greatest of these challenges was the recovery of American life and culture from the fanatical fringe. According to his biographer Edward Wagenknecht, "He was of the stuff of which martyrs are made, yet he had none of the fanaticism commonly associated with martyrs."[176] He was not extremist enough for most of his critics but had a tireless gift for compromise and adjustment. Indeed, he had what he called, "a Greek horror of extremes."[177] As Henry Cabot Lodge said of him:

*He held to the golden middle course, not
tepidly or timorously, but with the zeal and
conviction of a crusader. He was a middle-of-
the-road man, not because he was unwilling or
afraid of committing himself to the position on
either side, but he found the way to truth to lie
midway between the two extremes. He was a
zealot and fighter for truth, justice, and righteousness. He found no monopoly of any one of
these precious possessions in the camp of
extremists on either side. He found moderation
the one virtue everyone wished to ignore.*[178]

And so he became a champion of the ordinary concern.
He became a spokesman for the common man. He became an
advocate for the everyday affair. He did so because he was
gripped by the truth of Edmund Burke's famous truism, "The
only thing necessary for the triumph of evil is for good men
to do nothing."[179]

He entered politics, because he saw a need–not because
he saw an opportunity. He plunged into every great task–
reforming the civil service, blocking the manipulations of the
political machines, restructuring the criminal justice system,
reinvigorating the military establishment, and reinventing the
political campaign–because of a sense of calling and a sense
of duty to simply do what was right:

*The foes of our own household are our worst
enemies; and we can oppose them, not only by
exposing them and denouncing them, but by
constructive work in planning and building
reforms which shall take into account both the
economic and the moral factors in human
advance.*[180]

He had nothing but contempt for those who knew what was right, but failed to act. He could not stand the idea that people might suggest a course of action for others that they themselves were not willing to take. He himself was an undoubted intellectual, but he reserved only enmity for the indolence of the ivory tower.

He read Cotton Mather's famous monograph, *To Do Good*, at least a dozen times–more than any other book besides Walter Scott's *Waverley* and John Bunyan's *Pilgrim's Progress*. That great colonial Puritan credo became his moral beacon light. He believed that the future of American civilization fully depended upon faithful men translating their good intentions into good deeds:

> *We in America can attain our great destiny*
> *only by service; not by rhetoric, and above all*
> *not by insincere rhetoric, and that dreadful*
> *mental double-dealing and verbal juggling*
> *which makes promises and repudiates them,*
> *and says one thing at one time, and the directly*
> *opposite thing at another time. Our service*
> *must be the service of deeds.*[181]

To his mind, true leadership was the ability to model for the people a pattern of behavior that was not content to deal in mere purposes and intentions. For him, true leadership was always intent on exposing the hypocrisy of believing one thing and doing another. True leadership was a life committed to good deeds.

REFORMER

I believe in waging relentless war on rank-growing evils of all kinds.[182]

The role of the reformer is one of the most difficult and dangerous in all of civic life–especially if the reformer resists the urge to embrace all extremes and holds to the conservative course of balance and moderation. Theodore Roosevelt discovered this hard truth early on in his political career:

> *It is not always easy to keep the just middle, especially when it happens that on one side are corrupt and unscrupulous demagogues, and on the other side corrupt and unscrupulous reactionaries.*[183]

During his first term as a state legislator in New York, he ran into trouble with the political bosses almost immediately upon arriving in Albany. On the floor of the Assembly he had issued a clarion call for an investigation into the corrupt judicial and civil service systems–much to the dismay of those whose vested interests might be threatened by such an investigation. They decided to teach him a lesson. One night as he was leaving a hotel buffet where legislators met after hours to discuss various issues, he was confronted by a noisy crowd of well-to-do businessmen and raconteurs. Among them was an infamous boxer named "Stubby" Collins. The pugilist proceeded to jostle Roosevelt with some force–and with a great show of indignation, demanded that the young legislator apologize for "running in to him." But then, without waiting for his reply, Collins took a swipe at him. Roosevelt, now realizing that the throng of businessmen had hired the thug to beat him up, prepared to defend himself. The fight lasted less than a minute. Collins had more than met his match. As several astonished bystanders helped the badly beaten boxer off the floor, Roosevelt walked across the lobby and pleasantly informed the promoters of the affair that he understood their connection with it, and was greatly obliged to them. "I have not enjoyed anything so much for a year," he said. And with that, he made his way out into the night.

With such pluck and aplomb, Roosevelt always faced his opposition. He did not expect his reforms to be received without the howls and groans of political conflict. Nevertheless he never shied away from a fight. "Right is right and wrong is wrong, " he asserted. "Woe be unto the man who shies away from the battle for justice and righteousness simply because the minions of injustice and unrighteousness are arrayed against him." [184]

And so, throughout his career Roosevelt was forever sticking his nose into affairs that more cautious politicians had always done their utmost to leave alone–labor relations, tax reform, racial reconciliation, conservationism, monopolization, civil rights, eugenics, segregation, abortion, bureaucratic inefficiency, and judicial corruption. For him, it was simply a matter of calling.

But for a man who was so driven by a sense of justice and righteousness, he was surprisingly practical. He understood how the game of politics worked. He was not adverse to the give and take of political negotiation. He knew the value of the art of compromise and he practiced it–as long as his compromises never diminished his principles. He was a coalition builder. He kept his eye on the prize, and was not overly concerned with the proprieties of party or partisanship as long as good ends were attained:

> *The important thing generally is the next step.*
> *We ought not to take it unless we are sure that*
> *it is advisable; but we should not hesitate to*
> *take it once we are sure; and we can safely join*
> *with others who also wish to take it, without*
> *bothering our heads overmuch as to any some-*
> *what fantastic theories that they may have*
> *concerning, say, the two hundredth step, which*
> *is not yet in sight.*[185]

This approach generally drove his opponents mad–partly because it was so successful, and partly because it was so unpredictable. But for Roosevelt such an approach was the very essence of leadership. His goal, first and foremost, was to reach the goal.

SOCIALISM

It is difficult to make our material condition better by the best of laws, but it is easy enough to ruin it by bad laws.[186]

*T*heodore Roosevelt was no friend of the great accumulators of wealth who dominated the worlds of politics, industry, and commerce in his day. From the beginning of his career, he confronted men like Jay Gould, J.P. Morgan, John D. Rockefeller, and Andrew Carnegie. He spearheaded a determined enforcement of the Sherman Anti-Trust Act to break the stranglehold of gargantuan monopolies and trusts on the American economy–thus earning the moniker, "the Trust Buster."[187]

Despite this, he was hardly a liberal–much less a socialist–in his economic views. He even wrote a book, entitled *The Foes of Our Own Household*, denouncing the whole concept of overly intrusive government interventionism in the daily affairs of life.

Essentially, he was simply determined to protect ordinary Americans against the "creeping dehumanization" of an ideological secularism that he believed was already beginning to

dominate the national life.[188] Roosevelt believed it necessary
to "employ a certain skepticism" [189] even at the expense of the
"cult" of science–which all too often looked rather innocent
and disinterested, but which was actually neither. Of course,
he was not at all resistant to science or technological
progress–in fact he took great glee in such. Instead, he was
resistant to the crass and inhuman humanism that often
accompanied the "industrial collectivization" of the "malefactors of great wealth." [190] He believed that any way of life that
"omits or de-emphasizes either the freedom or the responsibility of individuals and families" was "necessarily disastrous
to all dimensions of life and culture." [191]

As a result, he regarded socialism as well as monopolism,
democratic liberalism as well as communism, republican
cooperationism as well as nationalistic fascism, with equal
disdain.[192] In fact, he professed an "ingrained suspicion" of all
schemes that "proposed to coerce ordinary people" to their
"alleged benefit." [193] He was at heart, opposed to all manner of
utopianism–whether of the left or the right.

Affected by the thinking of the Distributists of Britain, the
Christian Democrats of Holland and the early Agrarians of
the South, Roosevelt took a position that essentially affirmed
the principles of free enterprise, small business ownership,
and open fair trade without embracing the corporatism, mercantilism, and uniformitarianism of monopolistic capitalism.
He feared that with the growth of American economic depen-
dency on the huge industrial combines, most men and
women were being reduced to a new kind of modern servile
status–what he called "industrial serfs."

What he advocated as an alternative was a proliferation
of new small business and property ownership. He did not
want Americans to become the unpropertied wards of a huge
messianic entity–be it the government or the corporation:

> *We are steadily bent on preserving the institu-*
> *tion of private property; we combat every*
> *tendency toward reducing the people to eco-*
> *nomic servitude; and we care not whether the*
> *tendency is due to a sinister agitation directed*
> *against all property, or whether it is due to the*
> *actions of those members of the predatory*
> *classes whose anti-social power is immeasur-*
> *ably increased because of the very fact that*
> *they possess wealth.* [194]

Nevertheless, he had little confidence in the agency of government to adequately address his concerns about consolidation. He was no starry-eyed liberal whose reform mantra was little more than "There ought to be a law." Instead, he remained more than a little suspicious of both the efficacy and the motivation of government social or economic programs. Indeed, were he to choose one or the other, he would always choose the private sector over the public as the best guarantor of freedom:

> *Under government ownership corruption can*
> *flourish just as rankly as under private owner-*
> *ship. I do not believe in government ownership*
> *of anything which can with propriety be left in*
> *private hands.* [195]

Roosevelt was an idealist—but he was also blessed with a strong dose of realism. He knew that there were no simple or easy solutions to the grave problems that faced America and the world. As a result, he was the rarest of all politicians: he distrusted the ultimate efficacy of idealistic and ideological politics.

THE BULLY PULPIT

The White House is a bully pulpit.[196]

*U*pon leaving the White House, Roosevelt declined an offer to sit on the board of a large corporation at a salary of $100,000 a year–an enormous amount of money at the time. Instead he accepted the position of associate editor of the Outlook magazine–a small but highly regarded journal of cultural and political thought–at a salary of $12,000 a year. He told friends that he chose the better job. "I am far more interested in the influence I might be able to wield," he said, "speaking my heart and mind to the nation than I am in money or power."[197]

Throughout his life he considered his greatest contributions to American life to be those times when he spoke directly to the people. He was committed to politics and to the processes of government. But he knew only too well the grave limitations that the system imposed on real and substantive change. On the other hand, he had supreme confidence in the people to make wise decisions and to take appropriate actions–if only they were given the right information and the right opportunities.

Thus, he was vigilant in his efforts to communicate. He was the first President to effectively use the press to his own political advantage. Every other chief executive only had tolerated journalists and photographers. Roosevelt embraced them. He gave them two short briefings every day. He kept them informed of his meetings, agendas, and policies. He made them an integral part of his overall political strategy.

In addition, Roosevelt was the first president to travel extensively to every section of the country. In his first administration alone, he made thirty-five trips outside of Washington—including an extensive tour of the South and a 45,000 mile journey from coast to coast. At every whistle-stop, at every historical site, at every major city, and at every scenic locale along the way, he mingled with the people, made speeches, and honored local dignitaries. He always did research on the local traditions, distinctives, and customs, and then mentioned such in his speeches. In so doing, he not only wove an intricate grassroots web of personal support, he put his stamp on the local consciousness. He earned the right to speak into their lives—because he came to them not as an outsider, but as a compatriot.

He was born in the Northeast—and so had a natural affinity with the people there. But he made his name in the West—so the people in that region claimed him as his own. His maternal family line was one of the most distinguished in the old South—and he made good use of those connections as well. Indeed, he could lay claim to being the first president whose support entirely transcended regionalism and parochialism. And he unashamedly used that tremendous advantage to advance his various political causes and positions.

All of this was a part of Roosevelt's determined strategy to use the White House as a "bully pulpit." It was his very deliberate attempt to bypass the gridlock of politics as usual, and instead take his message directly to the people.

Because he believed that the role of the leader was primarily to serve as a moral compass–pointing the nation toward the true north of justice and righteousness–he took every opportunity to inform them, to encourage them, to exhort them, to reprove them, to stimulate them, and to inspire them. He dedicated every high school, opened every bridge, presided at every anniversary, visited every monument, and convened every convention he possibly could. His pulpit was employed with an evangelist's fervor:

> *We must diligently strive to make our young men decent, God-fearing, law-abiding, honor-loving, justice-doing, and also fearless and strong, able to hold their own in the hurly-burly of the world's work, able to strive mightily that the forces of right may be in the end triumphant. And we must be ever vigilant in so telling them.*[198]

His presidential addresses and speeches alone would eventually comprise seven thick volumes–a prodigious output, especially considering the fact that he used no speech writers. But Roosevelt believed that such herculean labors were an essential component of his leadership task:

> *The man who knows the truth and has the opportunity to tell it, but who nonetheless refuses to, is among the most shameful of all creatures. God forbid that we should ever become so lax as that.*[199]

The Common Man

*The nameless pioneers and settlers, the obscure
mothers and fathers, the quiet craftsmen and trades-
men; it is only among these that the real story of
America is told; it is only among them that the bril-
liance of liberty may be comprehended.*[200]

*I*n his book, *Hero Tales from American History*,
Theodore Roosevelt chose to profile a number of little known individuals and incidents. It was in the ordinary
conduct of ordinary lives in ordinary circumstances that he
believed "the genius of the American civilization" was most
effectively made known.[201]

He believed that it was a noble pursuit to remind people–
especially, to remind young people–of the men and women of
the past "who showed that they knew how to live and how to
die; who proved their truth by their endeavor."[202] And more
often than not, the best exemplars of such heroic virtue were
not the famous or the prominent, but the forgotten and the
obscure.

And so, he gave much of his life to helping people
remember, cherish, and protect the glorious accomplishments
of the common man.

G.K. Chesterton–one of Roosevelt's favorite contemporary writers–often asserted that, "The most extraordinary thing in the world is an ordinary man and an ordinary woman and their ordinary children." [203] Ultimately that is one of the great lessons of history. It is that ordinary people are the ones who determine the outcome of human events in the end–not kings and princes, not masters and tyrants. It is laborers and workmen, cousins and acquaintances that upend the expectations of the brilliant and the glamorous, the expert and the meticulous. It is plain folks, simple people, who literally change the course of history–because they are the stuff of which history is made. They are the ones who make the world go round.

In his years on the western range, during his battles to reform the civil service system and the police department, on the field of battle with the Rough Riders, and throughout his many campaigns, Roosevelt had come to have a deep and abiding admiration for the workaday citizens who faithfully tended their gardens, raised their children, perfected their trades, and minded their businesses. He had become utterly convinced that in America the heroic could be found more readily in the mundane than in the profane, that glory might be discovered more obviously in commonness than in prominence, and that the least and the last were, in truth, the first and the foremost.

Jacob Riis claimed that by championing this peculiarly unmodern conception in both politics and life, Roosevelt has left an extraordinary cultural legacy to the nation he loved so dearly:

> *He knew well the importance of history, of*
> *remembering the great and mighty deeds of the*
> *past. But he knew equally well the importance*
> *of remembering what was actually important*

in history; of discerning what were in truth the
great and mighty deeds; of retaining that which
may be neglected by the text books, but must
never be by the ordinary citizen. He therefore
unashamedly staked his claim with the com-
mon man.[204]

As a result of this remarkable conviction, he consciously chose to rearrange his priorities so that his daily schedule might better reflect his true principles–even when that proved to be a source of profound irritation to the rich, famous, and powerful men around him.

For instance, he often postponed serious affairs of state in order to converse with average citizens. Once, he left two senators, five congressmen, and the heads of seven major corporations to wait in the White House for two hours while he discussed flora and fauna with a half dozen truck farmers from Alabama. When he finally showed the influential men into his office, one of the senators sternly rebuked him, "Mr. President, you must stand by your priorities." To which Roosevelt responded, "Oh, but I did, Senator. I did."

On another occasion, he slipped out of a very dull, but apparently important, diplomatic reception at the German Embassy to watch the last few innings of a baseball game. When the White House press corps caught up with him, they asked if he was not concerned that his actions might cause the German Empire to take offense. He replied, "I'm more concerned that this local nine might take offense–since I missed the first five innings of their championship match." [205]

Roosevelt knew that what was really important in life rarely put on airs of importance. And ultimately, he believed that this was the surest test of true leadership in a free republic.

HUMILITY

*I am just an ordinary man, without any special abil-
ity in any direction.*[206]

*D*espite his prodigious learning, his prolific accomplishments, and his popular fame, Roosevelt
remained unaffected. Throughout his life he was forthrightly
modest. Though he was the most dominating public figure of
his time, he consistently maintained that he was not a great
man:

> *In most things I am just about average; in some
> of them a little under, rather than over. I am
> only an ordinary walker. I can't run. I am not a
> good swimmer, although I am a strong one. I
> probably ride better than anything else I do, but
> I am certainly not a remarkably good rider. I
> am not a good shot. I never could be a good
> boxer, although I do keep at it, whenever I can.
> My eyesight prevents me from ever being a good
> tennis player, even if otherwise I could qualify.*

> *I am not a brilliant writer. I have written a*
> *great deal, but I always have to work and slave*
> *over everything I write. The things I have done*
> *are all, with the possible exception of the*
> *Panama Canal, just such things as any ordi-*
> *nary man could have done. There is nothing*
> *brilliant or outstanding in my record at all.*[207]

This was not false modesty. Nor was it self-disparagement. It was, he believed, instead a genuine and honest assessment of his abilities. When he compared himself to the great men of the past–his own heroes from American history–he always felt he came up lacking.

Roosevelt very consciously and consistently sought to apply the virtue of humility in his life. He tried to see himself in the light of truth. He carefully practiced the Christian principle of self-examination.

For example, often before retiring to bed, Roosevelt, and his friend the naturalist William Beebe, would step outside the White House and look up into the night sky, searching for a tiny patch of light near the constellation Pegasus. "That is the Spiral Galaxy in Andromeda," they would chant in unison. "It is as large as our Milky Way. It is one of a hundred million galaxies. It consists of one hundred billion suns, each larger than our own sun." After a moment of silent awe, Roosevelt would then turn to his companion and say, "Now I think we are small enough. Let's go to bed." [208]

Roosevelt was quite impatient with the sycophants who cluttered his private life and fawned over him in public. "I don't care a rap for popularity," he would often quip.[209] And he was utterly indifferent to presidential protocol. He could never get used to being served first at meals in the White House and he violently objected to ladies rising in his presence. After all, he believed that the commonplace things of ordinary mannerliness and human relations took precedence over all issues of office or position.

His sense of what was truly impressive in life also greatly contributed to his stunning humility:

> *There are two kinds of success. One is the very*
> *rare kind that comes to the man who has the*
> *power to do what no one else has the power to*
> *do. That is genius. Whether it is the genius of*
> *the man who can write a poem that no one*
> *else can write, The Ode on a Grecian Urn, for*
> *example, or Helen, Thy Beauty Is to Me; or of a*
> *man who can do one hundred yards in nine*
> *and three-fifths seconds; only a very limited*
> *amount of the success of life comes to persons*
> *possessing genius. The average man who is suc-*
> *cessful—the average statesman, the average*
> *public servant, the average soldier, who wins*
> *what we call success—is not a genius. He is a*
> *man who has merely the ordinary qualities that*
> *he shares with his fellows, but who has devel-*
> *oped those ordinary qualities to a more than*
> *ordinary degree.*[210]

There can be little doubt that Roosevelt would have preferred to be known in history as an average man rather than a genius. He would have much rather been known as a man who developed his ordinary qualities to a more than ordinary degree. His motto was simply, "Do what you can, with what you've got, where you are."[211]

There is little extraordinary about the achievements of a genius, a prodigy, or a savant. Inevitably, a great leader is someone who overcomes tremendous obstacles and still succeeds. Thus did Theodore Roosevelt succeed–overcoming a sickly childhood, personal tragedy, and fierce opposition from the vested interests–to lead the world with unmatched vision and valor.

His son Kermit truthfully could confess, "Father had no sense of his own greatness, only of the greatness of opportunity that each of us has." [212]

WAR AND PEACE

A just war is in the long run far better for a man's soul than the most prosperous peace.[213]

Critics of Theodore Roosevelt often found it difficult to oppose a man of such immense popularity, unbounded energy, and unmatched competency. He was practically immune to the ordinary discourse of political contention. The only tactic with which they found consistent success was to accuse him of reckless impetuousness, ambitious adventurism, and hot-headed war mongering in the all too delicate area of international affairs.

To be sure, Roosevelt was plain-spoken in his pronouncements about the advantages of war and the dangers of peace in certain circumstances:

> *The things that will destroy America are prosperity-at-any-price, peace-at-any-price, safety-first instead of duty-first, the love of soft living, and the get-rich-quick theory of life.*[214]

Though he had seen the horrors of war firsthand, he maintained a romantic image of its manly rectitude:

> *No qualities called out by a purely peaceful life stand on a level with those stern and virile virtues which move the men of stout heart and strong hand who uphold the honor of their flag in battle.*[215]

Indeed, he felt that a willingness to go to war for a just cause was a kind of litmus test of its integrity and honor:

> *A nation is not wholly admirable unless in times of stress it will go to war for a great ideal.*[216]

Conversely, his view of peace–particularly the sort of peace-at-any-price that many isolationists advocated–was all too often a misnomer for something less than a shameful betrayal of all that the American experiment in liberty stood for:

> *Peace is generally good in itself, but it is never the highest good unless it comes as the hand-maiden of righteousness; and it becomes a very evil thing if it serves merely as a mask for cowardice and sloth, or as an instrument to further the ends of despotism or anarchy.*[217]

Quite naturally, many men and women across the country feared that once he attained the office of the presidency, the nation would be perpetually mired in one misbegotten military adventure after another. But of course, that simply was not the case. In fact, the two Roosevelt administrations were among the most peaceful and harmonious in all of American history. And as if that were not enough, the president was awarded the Nobel Peace Prize for his role in negotiating the end to the bitter Russo-Japanese War in 1905– the first American so honored.

A reporter once asked the former president about this paradox. He kiddingly replied, "I certainly would never have started a war I couldn't have fought in." [218] In truth, Roosevelt's military policy was designed to enforce peace through strength:

> *I only advocate preparation for war in order to*
> *avert war; and I should never advocate war*
> *itself unless it were the only possible alterna-*
> *tive to shame and dishonor.*[219]

In 1908, he commissioned a complete American battle fleet under the command of Admiral Robert Evans to circle the globe. The ships were painted a brilliant white for their 42,000-mile show of force. Though critics were appalled at such blatant saber rattling, Roosevelt contended that the famed "Great White Fleet" had "exercised a greater influence for peace than all the peace conferences of the last fifty years." [220]

He believed that the essence of leadership was the ability to maintain great strength without any impulsive compulsion to use it. That strength was to be held in reserve until, and unless, it became necessary to use for the cause of right:

> *I abhor unjust war. I abhor injustice and bully-*
> *ing by the strong at the expense of the weak,*

*whether among nations or individuals. I abhor
violence and bloodshed. But it takes strength to
put a stop to abhorrent things.*[221]

And so the peace was kept.

SCIENCE

The tracing of an unbroken line of descent from the
protozoan to Plato does not in any way really
explain Plato's consciousness.[222]

*T*heodore Roosevelt thought of himself as a man of
science. From childhood he immersed himself in the
accouterments and the ethos of a scientific life. Until his final
year in college he was planning to dedicate his full concerns
to scientific pursuits. Even after he launched into the career
trajectory of politics and journalism, he maintained a lively
interest and an active hand in scientific matters.

And his involvement was hardly amateurish. Academi-
cians, naturalists, and scientific specialists were continually
astonished at the depth of his insight and understanding. The
great ornithologist, Frank Chapman, claimed, "The President
knows more about birds than I do." [223] The South American
zoologist, Ferdinand Zahm, was amazed "by his broad and
exact knowledge of the flora and fauna of lands he had never
yet visited." [224] And the scientific historian, C. Hart Merriam,
,called him "the world's authority on the big game mammals
of North America." [225]

The Natural History Museum at the Smithsonian Institution once had a specimen of a prematurely born mammal which no one on the prestigious staff could identify. So they sent the specimen to the White House. Roosevelt not only identified it at once, but supplied the scientists with a tremendous amount of information that greatly expedited their researches.

On another occasion, he visited a laboratory at the museum where some five thousand skulls, in various stages of disarray, were being assembled by a crack team of experts. Roosevelt astonished everyone–including several eminent naturalists who were visiting the site–by picking up skull after skull and mentioning the scientific name of the genus to which each belonged.

On yet another occasion, a paleontologist mentioned to him a very obscure species of mouse that had recently been discovered in a remote section of northern British Columbia. He supposed that none but a very well-informed specialist would know anything about the rodent. But upon mention of it, Roosevelt immediately began to tell him all about it. He was perfectly familiar with the little animal.

But despite his minute familiarity with the natural sciences, he was not prone–as so many scientists are–to the fads and fancies of scientific inquiry. He did not believe that simply because technology made a thing possible, that it should necessarily be done. He did not accept the notion of unfettered progress simply for the sake of progress:

> *Progress has brought us both unbounded*
> *opportunities and unbridled difficulties. Thus,*
> *the measure of our civilization will not be that*
> *we have done much, but what we have done*
> *with that much. I believe that the next half*

> *century will determine if we will advance the*
> *cause of Christian civilization or revert to the*
> *horrors of brutal paganism.*[226]

The proper use of scientific knowledge and advancement was a supremely moral concern for him:

> *The thought of modern industry in the hands of*
> *Christian charity is a dream worth dreaming.*
> *The thought of industry in the hands of pagan-*
> *ism is a nightmare beyond imagining. The*
> *choice between the two is upon us.*[227]

Additionally, he was not susceptible to the smothering uniformity of scientific theorizing. Though he was comfortable with certain aspects of evolutionary theory, he was an outspoken critic of Darwinism–delivering several important papers challenging the unquestioning faith of many scientists in the theory. When he delivered the Romanes Lectures at Oxford University, he highlighted "the fallacy of using parallels between the evolution of animal life and the development of human societies and glib attempts to apply Darwinism to social development." [228]

He believed that science–like politics–was merely a tool or a resource to be used for the good of mankind–not an end unto itself. And its limitations and inadequacies were always to be kept in full view.

He believed that a wise leader always uses whatever resources are placed at his disposal–but he never confused the means with the ends.

THE SOUTH

I can quite legitimately claim to be a proud son of the South.[229]

*T*he wounds of the War between the States were still aching and raw when Theodore Roosevelt arrived in the White House. It had only been twenty-five years since the end of Reconstruction, and the bitterness between North and South remained unabated. And although the Spanish-American War had had an enormous unifying effect on certain portions of both regions, the nation was still scarred by a great emotional, cultural, and economic divide.

Roosevelt was the first president to self-consciously cross that divide. His paternal relations were all Northern unionists, through and through. But all his maternal relations were thoroughly unreconstructed Southerners. And so he was actually able to embrace the best of both traditions.

The Bulloch family of Roswell, Georgia, boasted a member of the Continental Congress, the first governor of Georgia, and a brigadier general in the Continental Army. Their plantation home, Bulloch Hall, was one of the most magnificent in the South, and the hub of the region's social, political, and cultural relations. Margaret Mitchell, who wrote about the house early in her career as an Atlanta newspaper reporter, used it as the model for Tara in her novel *Gone With the Wind.*[230]

Two of Roosevelt's Bulloch uncles served with distinction in the Navy of the Confederate States of America. James Dunwoodie Bulloch, at the outbreak of hostilities between North and South, was a captain in the merchant marine. His ship was in port at New Orleans at the time of the secession of Louisiana from the Union, and the governor demanded the vessel be handed over to the state. Bulloch refused–he believed honor required him to deliver the vessel into the hands of her owners in New York. As soon as he had fulfilled his obligations, however, Bulloch presented himself to President Jefferson Davis for service to his country. He was immediately commissioned a captain in the fledgling navy. He became one of the most successful blockade runners in the South. Later he was sent to England to buy and equip vessels of war. The British government was forbidden by the laws of neutrality to permit such a thing–but Captain Bulloch's ingenuity prevailed. He was eventually able to set sail at least a half dozen ships under the Confederate stars and bars–including the warship, the *Alabama.*

Irvine Stephens Bulloch, the captain's younger brother, became the navigating officer of the *Alabama.* When that great ship was finally sunk in a savage sea battle off the coast of France, the young Bulloch commanded the last gun that was in action and fired the last shot from her sinking deck. After the war, seeing their national cause utterly lost, both men chose to live out their lives in exile, rather than submit to the humiliation of the devastating Reconstruction years.

Many of Theodore Roosevelt's fondest memories as a child were of visits to his two uncles in England. They regaled him with stories of the old South. They filled his mind with the sense of honor, filial duty, and undying valor that so marked the ideals of the Confederacy. And though he did not share their attachment to the doctrines of secession or servility, he never ceased to admire them and their legacy. He said that the two men, "always struck me as the nearest approach to genuine heroes of any men I ever met in actual life." [231]

During his administration, Roosevelt made a point of including portions of the South as an integral part of every presidential tour. He visited Roswell nearly a dozen times-always asserting his affectionate attachment to the place. He completely altered the civil service system in the South-which had been by far the most corrupt in the nation since the time of Reconstruction-even to the point of appointing qualified Democrats rather than keeping the heirs of the carpetbaggers and scalawags on the federal dole. He often requested *Dixie*-which he considered "the best of all our national tunes"-to be played at various state dinners. [232]

By modern standards, these may not seem to be particularly innovative measures. But at the turn of the century they were considered extraordinary reforms.

Roosevelt set out to unite the disparate and distinctive legacies of North and South in the same way they had been united in his own family. And in so doing, he helped the nation begin the vital process of healing-at long last.

HUMOR

*T*here is nothing in a leader at once so sane and so sympathetic as a good sense of humor. That Theodore Roosevelt was possessed of prodigious jocularity, there can be little doubt.

According to Henry Cabot Lodge, "No man ever had a more abundant sense of humor–joyous, irrepressible humor–and it never deserted him. Even at the most serious and perilous moments if there was a gleam of humor anywhere, he saw it and rejoiced and helped himself with it over the rough places and in the dark hour." [233]

He loved fun. He loved to joke. And he loved silly pranks. As Lodge said, "His ready smile and contagious laugh made countless friends and saved him from many an enmity." [234]

Perhaps best of all, Roosevelt could laugh at himself–and there was plenty to laugh at. Because of his furious activity, he was constantly injuring himself. He obviously was not a clumsy man, and yet throughout his life he broke at least 19 bones. And he endured more cuts, scrapes, bruises, and injuries than can be imagined, much less than can be counted. He dislocated a knee while chasing the children down the White House stairs. He suffered a concussion during a contraband football match in the Blue Room. And he was blinded in one eye during a boxing match with the former heavyweight champion of the world in the new executive offices' wing. Roosevelt saw the absurdity in this–and was often the first to burst out into laughter following one of his mishaps.

In addition though, he had the ability to laugh right along with his political critics at his foibles, faux pas, and failures. He always enjoyed political cartoons–even when the joke came at his own expense. And though he was scathing in his denunciations of yellow journalism, he never failed to appreciate the humor in political satire.

When people met him for the first time, invariably they would be impressed by his ready laugh and ear-to-ear grin. He had a very personable way of breaking down barriers and inhibitions with his infectious good humor. A fierce political opponent once said that, "The problem with meeting with Roosevelt face to face is that you have to go in hating him an awful lot not to come out liking him even more." [235]

Wit was such an important part of his stump personae that several newspapers around the country began running a weekly column containing only jokes and humorous anecdotes from his speeches. The famed humor writer, Homer Davenport, asserted:

> *Theodore Roosevelt is a humorist. In the multitude of his strenuousness this, the most human of his accomplishments, has apparently been overlooked. There is a similarity between his humor and Mark Twain's. If Roosevelt were on the vaudeville stage he would be a competitor of Harry Lauder. No one can sit through one of*

his speeches with a straight face. He can make
a joke as fascinating as he can the story of a
sunset on the plains of Egypt.[236]

According to Jacob Riis, this "comic genius was simply the result of a happy life." [237] He loved life. He had fun. And he never took himself or any of his accomplishments too terribly seriously.

During the most difficult days of the 1912 campaign, when he was forced to take on both major established parties with no real political organization, a meager budget, and a hodgepodge staff, his happy disposition and good humor is nearly all that kept the Progressives afloat. His light-hearted attitude toward "Hudge" (Wilson) and "Pudge" (Taft) kept his frustrated and discouraged volunteers in stitches. One of those workers later recalled:

> *Some may remember Roosevelt for his legisla-*
> *tive accomplishments. Others for his literary*
> *feats. Still others for his moral courage. But I*
> *will always remember him for his ability to*
> *take any circumstance and see it through the*
> *lens of happy providence. He was, for me, living*
> *proof of the fact that laughter is indeed, the*
> *best medicine.*[238]

Courage

My success so far has only been won by absolute indifference to my future career.[239]

*H*ow can you describe the courage of Theodore Roosevelt other than to simply say it was inexhaustible. The instances of his physical and moral valor are almost too numerous to mention.

His experiences on the Western range would be enough to rank him among the nation's most courageous men. He not only tamed the wilds of the frontier, he tamed the wild frontiersmen–capturing fugitives, domesticating renegades, and besting ruffians. In Africa he calmly dropped a rhinoceros in full charge at fifty paces. Once he killed a mountain lion, while he was hanging over a cliff, head downwards, with his guide holding on to his feet.

In battle Roosevelt was utterly fearless–charging up San Juan Hill under a withering fire from entrenched enemy positions. Years later when he had become commander in chief, he never asked his men to do anything he was not willing to do himself. And so he went up in a box-kite airplane, went down in a primitive submarine, flew in a zeppelin, and drove in an overland half-track.

He took his duty as president as a kind of pastoral charge. Before the day of fly-by helicopters and presidential jets, he visited the sites of disasters, storms, fires, and floods to comfort and encourage the victims. "I am going to New Orleans," he once wrote to his son Kermit, during a particularly dire epidemic. "I believe the danger is infinitesimal, and I do not think a President ought ever, by his action, to give any chance to timid people to use his example as an excuse for their timidity." [240]

But as great as his physical courage obviously was, his moral courage was even greater. When he took on New York's corrupt political bosses single-handedly at the very beginning of his career, his enemies ridiculed him as a kid-gloved reformer. When he criticized Wilson's wartime policies at the very end of his career, he was condemned as an old has-been embittered with sour grapes. Neither reaction caused him to swerve for an instant from the course he had determined was right and good and true.

Whenever he had something unpleasant to say, he always seemed to find a way to say it to the most unsympathetic audience–he stated his commitment to the gold standard in the heart of the pro-silver belt; he defended the rigid New York blue laws in a downtown saloon district; he publicly rebuked the governor of Arkansas, sitting on the platform next to him, because he had implicationally defended racist lynchings; he condemned the rebels against British rule in an address in Cairo, though he had been warned that he would be shot if he even brought up the issue; and he received his friend Booker T. Washington on a dais in Jackson, Mississippi.

Time after time, establishment political operatives attempted to warn him against such impolitic maneuvers. But he was resolute. Anything less than absolute forthrightness, he considered a cowardly accommodation to office-holding–which was the very negation of true statesmanship:

> *I do not believe that any man should ever attempt to make politics his only career. It is a dreadful misfortune for a man to grow to feel that his whole livelihood and whole happiness depend upon his staying in office. Such a feeling prevents him from being of real service to the people while in office and always puts him under the heaviest strain of pressure to barter his convictions for the sake of holding office.* [241]

His boldness on the stump then, was a kind of personal insurance against compromise. The efficacy of his leadership depended, he believed, on his incognizance of the negative consequences of doing right. According to his friend Owen Wister, "He was indifferent to the outcome of a battle so long as he knew that he was on the right side, had given his all-in-all, and had had a bully time in the process." [242]

FAILURE

There is no disgrace in a failure, only in a failure to try.[243]

*T*heodore Roosevelt was never afraid to fail. In fact, he often wore his failures as badges of honor. To him, the attempt, the effort, and the sheer pluck of involvement was what really mattered in the end:

> *Far better it is to dare mighty things, to win glorious triumphs, even though checkered by failure, than to take rank with those poor spirits who neither enjoy much nor suffer much because they live in the gray twilight that knows neither victory nor defeat.*[244]

Though he enjoyed many successes throughout his career, he had his share of failures. He never allowed failure to stymie his sense of responsibility and calling. He was often knocked down, but never out.

In addition, he was eager to learn from his mistakes. Once, when his administration had lost a strategic legislative

battle on the floor of the Senate, he called each of the men
who had led the opposition to the White House. Expecting an
angry tirade or an hysterical harangue, the senators were surprised when Roosevelt anxiously gathered them around his
desk and asked for their advice. "How could I have handled
this bill better? What did I say or not say to cause you to
oppose it? What should I do in the future to better advance
my principles?" [245] The men were stunned. There was no
recrimination. There were no lectures. There were no threats.
Instead, they found in the president an eager learner–ready to
accept the blame for his own shortcomings and then to try to
move on and do better on another day. One of them later confessed, "I learned more about leadership and greatness in that
one incident than in all my previous years in politics." [246]

Elihu Root, who served as Roosevelt's secretary of state,
called him "the most advisable man I ever knew." [247] John Hay,
who designed the "Open Door" policy with China following
the Boxer Rebellion, often marveled at the "amiability and
open-mindedness" with which he accepted advice.[248] "If he
was convinced of your sincerity," said the Progressive leader
Albert Beveridge, "you could say anything to him you liked.
You could even criticize him personally." [249] And the author
and social reformer Herbert Croly remarked that he had
"never met a man so eager to learn from his mistakes–or
even so ready to admit them. It was as if he had no ego." [250]

Just a month after the defeat of the Progressive ticket in
1912, when others were still licking their wounds, he was
already analyzing, critiquing, and planning. His son Kermit
observed:

> *There are no full stops for him, no final defeats,*
> *and no ultimate victories. It seems that he is*
> *able to absorb every act of providence–be it*

> *good or bad from a human perspective–as one*
> *more necessary lesson in life. He is always*
> *growing, always learning, and always striving to*
> *make a better showing next time around. Each*
> *failure is for him merely an incomplete task*
> *along the way toward an ultimate success.*[251]

Roosevelt was not simply a hopeless romantic or an unrealistic optimist in this regard. Rather he was a man who was secure enough in his calling and purpose in life to remain undeterred by obstacles along the way–be they great or small. Again, Kermit explained:

> *Some men have a strong sense of destiny. I can-*
> *not say that Father could ever fully identify*
> *such sentiments in his own experience. But I*
> *am quite certain that he knew what to work*
> *toward. Whether he ever actually attained to it*
> *was another matter altogether–and one of little*
> *concern to him.*[252]

For Roosevelt, true leadership not only involved a strength of character that was unafraid to admit failure, was willing to learn from error, and was quick to accept wise counsel, it also involved a sense of calling that was able to integrate such virtues into life with real confidence. For him, failure was the backdoor to success.

FRIENDSHIP

*It may be true that he travels farthest who travels
alone; but the goal thus reached is not worth
reaching.*[253]

*T*heodore Roosevelt was a man of enormous social
skills. He had a compelling personal charisma that
naturally drew others to himself. He was affable, gregarious,
charming, and gracious. John Cater Rose once remarked that
"He gave every man he had talked with for five minutes the
impression that he liked him very much." [254]

He was a fascinating conversationalist. He was so
remarkably well-informed that he could speak intelligently
about almost any subject at length. But he by no means dominated discussions. Indeed, he was an avid listener who often
remained rather quiet in large public settings. He had a knack
for bringing out the best in others. Thus, according to Albert
Schauffler:

> *Though a brilliant, humorous, high-powered
> talker, he was more ear than mouth. On the*

*slightest indication that another had anything
to contribute, he would jam on all his verbal
brakes. He was perhaps the most creative listener I have ever encountered. If we all had
such audiences, we would continually excel
ourselves.*[255]

He was a great encourager. He liked nothing better than
to see others succeed. He marveled, even reveled, in the man-
ifest gifts of others. And he was abundantly profusive in his
praise of their achievements. As Irvin Cobb put it, "You had to
hate Roosevelt a whole lot to keep from loving him." [256]

As a result, he was a great friend—and he attracted a great
variety of intimates. From his schooldays at Harvard, he maintained lifelong friendships with such men of culture and
refinement as William Roscoe Thayer, Harry Shaw, and Minot
Weld. From his years in the West, he maintained long-term
relationships with rough and tumble cowboys like Bill Sewall,
Will Dow, and Bill Merrifield. From the world of politics, he
gained the devotion of cunning strategists like Elihu Root,
John Hay, and Henry Cabot Lodge. He was close to a number
of scientists—John Muir, C. Hart Merriam, and William Beebe;
military men—Fitzhugh Lee, Leonard Wood, George Dewey;
and writers—Jacob Riis, Rudyard Kipling, and Owen Wister. All
of them treasured his company and companionship as among
the most significant in their lives.

He was loyal, compassionate, tender-hearted, and most of
all, fun. He always remembered names, special occasions, and
intimate details about conversations that made his friends
feel a sense of supreme importance.

Amazingly though, Roosevelt was not a particularly social
person. Though he dearly loved his friends, he always preferred a quiet night at home with Edith and the children to

anything or anyone else. He did not enjoy going out. He was not a "joiner."[257] And he was convinced that he was a poor "mixer."[258] He hated parties and social occasions–especially if he knew that he was to be the center of attention, which he almost always was. "Huge banquets and such" were "horrid functions" in his eyes.[259] He always felt that he would be "caught" by some dominating boor or "button-holed" by some dim acquaintance–and often begged Edith to keep an eye out to "rescue him" if necessary.[260] For the more frivolous activities of organized society he felt only contempt. "My own family, good book, a roaring fire, and a simple meal on the porch, now that is my idea of a bully social event."[261] Both he and Edith loathed staying in other people's homes. When he was traveling he much preferred what he called "an old fogey hotel."[262] And his favorite restaurants were "often rather disreputable hole in the wall joints."[263]

He was, in reality, an intensely private person. He had only a handful of genuinely close friends with whom he shared his most intimate concerns. Henry Cabot Lodge was one. Jacob Riis was another. And of course, he was entirely transparent with Edith and his children.

Like anyone who is constantly thrust into the public eye, he was able to maintain a wide circle of relationships through a generous application of the social graces. But he simultaneously guarded his private affairs, maintaining genuine intimacy only with those whom he could trust implicitly.

A Pro-Life Stalwart

Never will I sit motionless while directly or indi-rectly apology is made for the murder of the helpless.[264]

Theodore Roosevelt was convinced that the family was the fundamental cornerstone of society. Anything that eroded the family's strength or vitality, anything that sought to undermine its authority or integrity, and anything that subverted its holy purpose or virtue was a dastardly threat to everything that he held to be good and right and true.

In his State of the Union message in 1905, he highlighted his grave concern for America's deteriorating moral climate in general, and the family's diminished cultural relevance, saying:

The transformation of the family is one of the greatest sociological phenomena of our time; it is a social question of the first importance, of far greater importance than any merely politi-cal or economic question can be.[265]

He went on to describe a rather simple agenda for protecting the family against the encroachment of those men and women he called "the foes of our own household." [266] He said:

> *There are those who believe that a new modernity demands a new morality. What they fail to consider is the harsh reality that there is no such thing as a new morality. There is only one morality. All else is immorality. There is only true Christian ethics over against which stands the whole of paganism. If we are to fulfill our great destiny as a people, then we must return to the old morality, the sole morality.* [267]

His analysis was utterly scathing:

> *All these blatant sham reformers, in the name of a new morality, preach the old, old vice and self-indulgence which rotted out first the moral fiber and then even the external greatness of Greece and Rome.* [268]

In a very real sense, Roosevelt was the original family values social conservative.

It is not surprising then, that when a new wave of abortion advocates made their way onto the American scene and into the public arena, Roosevelt was one of their chief opponents–in fact, apart from the hierarchy of the Catholic church, he was one of their only opponents. [269]

He railed against their "frightful and fundamental immorality," calling their cause a submission "to coldness, to selfishness, to love of ease, to shrinking from risk, and to an utter and pitiful failure in sense of perspective." [270] As he argued:

*Artificially keeping families small inevitably
involves prenatal infanticide and abortion–
with all its pandering to self-indulgence, its
shirking of duties, and its enervation of
character.*[271]

But he did not simply hurl invectives their way–he acted.
He was instrumental in mobilizing Republicans, Democrats,
and Progressives against the awful specter of commercial
child-killing–building a solid coalition that was to resist the
siren's call of abortion for another three-quarters of a century.
As he said:

*The foes of our own household are our worst
enemies; and we can oppose them, not only by
exposing them and denouncing them, but by
constructive work in planning and building
reforms which shall take into account both the
economic and the moral factors in human
advance. We in America can attain our great
destiny only by service; not by rhetoric, and
above all not by insincere rhetoric, and that
dreadful mental double-dealing and verbal jug-
gling which makes promises and repudiates
them, and says one thing at one time, and the
directly opposite thing at another time. Our service must be the service of deeds.*[272]

He went on to assert:

*The most dangerous form of sentimental
debauch is to give expression to good wishes
on behalf of virtue while you do nothing about*

> *it. Justice is not merely words. It is to be trans-*
> *lated into living acts.*[273]

The infamous Margaret Sanger, who founded the vast Planned Parenthood abortion network, rightly saw Roosevelt as "a holdover from the old Christian religion," and thus a serious obstacle to her revolutionary program which called for "no gods and no masters."[274] She railed against him as "a disgraceful blight upon any modern scientific nation's intent to advance."[275]

For a leader who had staked his reputation and risked his career for the sake of traditional family values, that was high praise indeed. For no commendation can be greater than the condemnation of one's fiercest sworn enemies.

PROGRESSIVE

A great democracy must be progressive or it will soon cease to be a democracy.[276]

*A*t the turn of the century, the urgent problems brought on by dramatic changes in the social and cultural landscape–mass urbanization, rampant industrialization, dire triage, and sudden class dispossession–demanded immediate and innovative solutions. The Progressive movement was a cultural and political phenomenon that arose to offer such solutions.

At first, the movement was non-partisan and non-ideological. It was simply a coalition of reform-minded individuals who came from every walk of life and from every political persuasion imaginable. They were united only in their concern for such things as industrial safety, child-labor, tenement sanitation, building standards, property rights, food purity guidelines, commercial integrity, tax restructuring, family dispossession, and market monopolization.

According to Roosevelt, the credo of this diverse movement was fairly straightforward and simple:

> *It is our business to show that nine-tenths of*
> *wisdom consists in being wise in time. Woe to*
> *our nation if we let matters drift, if in our*
> *industrial and political life we let an*
> *unchecked and utterly selfish individualistic*
> *materialism riot to its appointed end. That end*
> *would be widespread disaster, for it would*
> *mean that our people would be sundered by*
> *those dreadful lines of division which are*
> *drawn when the selfish greed of the haves is set*
> *over against the selfish greed of the have-nots.*
> *There is but one way to prevent such a divi-*
> *sion, and that is to forestall it by the kind of*
> *movement in which we are now engaged.*[277]

The aim was not to reinvent politics–or even the existing political parties and structures–but to provide an impetus for cooperative and harmonious reform for the good of all:

> *Our movement is one of resolute insistence*
> *upon the rights and full acknowledgment of the*
> *duties of every man and every woman within*
> *this great land of ours. We war against the*
> *forces of evil, and the weapons we use are the*
> *weapons of right. We do not set greed against*
> *greed or hatred against hatred. Our creed is one*
> *that bids us to be just to all, to feel sympathy*
> *for all, and to strive for an understanding of*
> *the needs of all. Our purpose is to smite down*
> *wrong. But to those who have done the wrong*
> *we feel only the kindliest charity that is com-*
> *patible with causing the wrong to cease. We*
> *preach hatred to no man, and the spirit in*

which we work is as far removed from vindic-
tiveness as from weakness. We are resolute to
do away with the evil, and we intend to pro-
ceed with such wise and cautious sanity as will
cause the very minimum of disturbance that is
compatible with achieving our purpose.[278]

Under his dynamic leadership at home–and with the English Distributist writer Hilaire Belloc leading the charge abroad–the movement produced a powerful groundswell of united support for sweeping social, political, and economic reforms. Rights were secured for organized labor; political machines were called into account; civil rights were insured; health and safety standards were instituted; small commercial interests were protected; and massive corporate trusts were reined in.

Despite remarkable successes in achieving its immediate aims however, Progressivism was short lived–at least as a single united movement. With success came the inevitable bickering and backbiting. The movement quickly splintered into wildly divergent special interest factions. In America, once Roosevelt left his "bully pulpit" in the White House, Henry Cabot Lodge and Charles Lindbergh Sr. valiantly tried to carry on Progressivism's tradition–as informed by Christian conviction, patriotism, and family values. In Europe, once Belloc left his seat in the House of Commons, Cecil Chesterton and Maurice Baring likewise attempted to uphold Progressivism's Distributist legacy. In both cases however, the bulk of the once mighty movement began to dissipate.

The fact is, among the movement's disparate factions and interests, there were a large number of irreverent and impatient young radicals who were guided by a very different ideological standard: the revolutionary philosophies and ideals of the humanistic Enlightenment. They pushed the bulk of Progressivism into the fringes of Western politics and culture, establishing dozens of groups intent on the utter decimation of Christendom's vision of life, liberty, and the pursuit of happiness: the Mugwumps, the Anarchists, the Knights of Labor, the Grangers, the Single-Taxers, the Suffragettes, the International Workers of the World, the Populists, and the Communists. What had begun as a conservative social movement for reform had spun out of control and become the motley aggregation of liberal activism.

As Roosevelt quipped, "Every reform movement has a lunatic fringe." [279]

The lunatic fringe, more than any other factor, caused the sudden dissipation of Progressive influence following the defeat of its ticket in 1912. Roosevelt himself remained committed to the conservative ideals of the early movement, but he was forced to admit to the single greatest error of his storied career: he believed that he could carry the weight of the movement on his own considerable shoulders.

His failure to do so forced him to recognize the fact that social movements need far more than a gifted or popular leader. They need a consensus wrought by a common worldview and a common faith.

PREJUDICE

I should hang my head in shame if I were capable of discriminating against a man because he and I have different shades of skin.[280]

Roosevelt had an acute sense of justice, fairness, and propriety. Though he was often accused of being a jingo and an ethnic elitist, he actually despised all manner of discrimination. He found prejudice intolerable. And he simply could not fathom how anyone–much less a professing Christian–could condone rank racism.

At a time when public men–and especially politicians– were either reticent to discuss matters of race or altogether mum, he was startlingly forthright in his pronouncements:

The wise and honorable and Christian thing to do is to treat each black man and each white man on his merits as a man, giving him no more and no less than he shows he is worthy to have.[281]

He was convinced of the equality of all men–though certainly not of all cultures–and only asked that individuals adhere to the principles and precepts of Christendom in order to partake equally of the benefits of society:

> *Above all we must stand shoulder to shoulder,*
> *not asking as to the ancestry or creed of our*
> *comrades, but only demanding that they be in*
> *very truth Americans, and that we all work*
> *together, heart, hand, and head, for the honor*
> *and the greatness of our common country.*[282]

Once, when he was the police commissioner of New York, this equanimity was severely put to the test. A notorious German anti-Semite came to the city for a series of meetings. He was caught in quite a conundrum:

> *A great many of the Jews became alarmed and*
> *incensed about his speaking here, and called*
> *upon me to prevent it. Of course, I told them I*
> *could not–that the right of free speech must be*
> *maintained, and that unless he incited to riot,*
> *he would be allowed to speak against the Jews*
> *just as we should let Jews speak against*
> *Christians.*[283]

At the same time, his sense of justice would not allow him to leave the situation at that, so he very creatively stamped the impress of his moral tenor on the difficult circumstance:

> *On thinking it over, it occurred to me that there*
> *was one way in which I could undo much of*

*the mischief he was trying to do, and I directed
that so far as possible the policemen detailed to
protect him at his meetings should themselves
be Jews. This done, and Herr Ahlwardt delivered
his violent harangues against the men of
Hebrew faith, owing his safety to the fact that
he was scrupulously protected by men of the
very race which he was denouncing.*[284]

The great racial divide in America–then as now–was
between black and white. Roosevelt was among the first political figures to evidence an attitude of equality and a defense
of civil rights:

*It was my good fortune at Santiago to serve
beside black troops. A man who is good enough
to shed his blood for his country is good
enough to be given a square deal afterward.
More than that no man is entitled to, and less
than that no man shall have.*[285]

When he was president, he caused a furor when he
invited his friend Booker T. Washington to dine with him in
the White House. The renowned black educator was the
founder of the Tuskegee Institute in Alabama and was one of
the most eloquent public speakers in America. In addition, he
was well acquainted with Southerners of both races and was
a good judge of men. As a result, Roosevelt had relied upon
him for some time for advice in selecting candidates, both
black and white, to fill federal positions in the region. When
it was reported that the president and his wife had enter-
tained a black man in the White House–an historic first–a
wave of protests were touched off in both the North and the

South. The *Memphis Scimitar* termed the dinner "the most damnable outrage ever." [286] One Senator even asserted that the nation's capital had become "so saturated with the odor of the nigger that the rats have taken refuge in the stables." [287]

Rather naive on the whole issue, Roosevelt was quite surprised by the hostile reaction:

> *I had no thought whatever of anything save of having a chance of showing some little respect to a man whom I cordially esteem as a good citizen and a good American. The outburst of feeling is to me literally inexplicable. It does not anger me. As far as I am personally concerned I regard their attacks with the most contemptuous indifference, but I am very melancholy that such feeling should exist in such bitterly aggravated form.* [288]

In the end, Roosevelt stuck by his guns asserting with typical epigrammatic precision, "Better faithful than famous." [289]

HEROES

*A nation needs heroes. It needs examples of valor so
that it will know just how it ought to behave.*[290]

*R*oosevelt always had difficulty seeing himself as a
hero. But that was merely because he was modest. He certainly did not abide by the peculiarly modern
notion that men should cynically avoid heroes. He was particularly enamored with a large number of heroes from the
past:

> *From reading of the people I admired–ranging
> from the soldiers of Valley Forge and Morgan's
> riflemen to my Southern forefathers and kin-
> folk–I felt a great admiration for men who were
> fearless and who could hold their own in the
> world. And I had a great desire to be like
> them.*[291]

Many of his heroes were rather typical. He held George
Washington and Abraham Lincoln in great esteem, for
instance. He was also terribly fond of Alexander Hamilton,

Patrick Henry, Stonewall Jackson, Daniel Boone, Robert E. Lee, and George Rogers Clark.

In addition though, he greatly admired a number of rather less likely heroes. As an avid reader of Walter Scott's *Waverley* novels, he had developed a tremendous affection for William Wallace, Robert the Bruce, and Bonnie Prince Charlie. Scott's *Ivanhoe* was a personal favorite–and so he had long been intrigued with the Crusaders, particularly Richard the Lion-Hearted. He was also an unabashed admirer of England's most revered kings–including Arthur, Alfred the Great, and Henry V.

His research and writing had made him particularly fond of Gouverneur Morris, Thomas Hart Benton, and Oliver Cromwell–all of whom became subjects of his biographical labors. And of course, he fairly idolized the men who won the West–such as James Robertson, John Sevier, and Meriweather Lewis.

When he and Henry Cabot Lodge wrote their *Hero Tales from American History,* they said their only desire was "to tell in simple fashion the story of some Americans who showed that they knew how to live and how to die; who proved their truth by their endeavor; and who joined to the stern and manly qualities which are essential to the well-being of a masterful people the virtues of gentleness, of patriotism, and of lofty adherence to an ideal." [292]

Indeed, they argued:

> *It is a good thing for all Americans, and it is an*
> *especially good thing for all young Americans,*
> *to remember the men who have given their*
> *lives in war and peace to the service of their*
> *fellow countrymen, and to keep in mind the*
> *feats of daring and personal prowess done in*

*time past by some of the many champions of the
nation in the various crises of her history.*[293]

Lodge later recalled that Roosevelt was especially concerned to set out for ordinary Americans a model of patriotic
decorum by portraying the lives, careers, and achievements of
their greatest forebears:

> *He wanted all men to be able to readily ascer-
> tain the chief ingredients of greatness and
> valor. He wanted to illustrate how thrift, indus-
> try, obedience to law, fulfillment of duty, and
> intellectual cultivation are essential qualities
> in the makeup of any successful people. He
> wanted to provide others with heroes such as
> had heretofore faithfully guided him through
> the many shallows and shoals of his own life
> and career. He wanted all Americans to benefit
> as he had from the giants of valor.*[294]

Of course, Roosevelt's first and greatest hero was his own
father. Throughout his life he confessed that his chief aim was
to live up to the standard of honor, courage, and integrity that
had been established for him. Because of his relationship with
his father, Roosevelt had early come to understand that all
leaders must first be led. Because of his relationship with his
father, he had early come to understand that every hero must
have his own heroes.

He lived his life as a sincere imitator of the best attributes of others–and so became a model for all those who have
come after him.

BULL FEATHERS

*Profanity is the parlance of the fool. Why curse
when there is such a magnificent language with
which to discourse?*[295]

*E*veryone agreed that Theodore Roosevelt lived one of
the most colorful lives of his day. His activities were
colorful. His ideals were colorful. His behavior was colorful.
And he had a colorful vocabulary to match.

It seems that he took as much delight in the English language as he did everything else in life. And he made
extraordinary use of it. His gift of phrase making was an integral aspect of his personality. Not surprisingly, much of his
uniquely picturesque nomenclature–usually first uttered
entirely off the cuff–has passed into common usage. Thus, we
have "the larger good," "the square deal," "a straight shooter,"
"the hot potato," "the big stick," "mollycoddles and weaklings,"
"beaten to a frazzle," "the hat in the ring," "calling a spade a
spade," "weasel words," "malefactors of great wealth," "how the
west was won," "piffle pendants," and "strange bedfellows." [296]

He loved the art of neologism–making up new words to
suit new occasions, often by combining old words or by

transforming nouns into verbs. Thus, we have "muckraking," "logothete," "tangibilitate," "pucksterism," "Baptistification," "driveler," "impuritanism," "bibblebabble," "intelligentry," "taftisn't," "acadenemic," and "wilsonizing." [297] His imagination was so rich that General Leonard Wood often said that "he was so greedy for a proper expression of the truth that all the words in the dictionary were never enough for him." [298]

The one use of the language he could not tolerate, however, was profanity. According to his closest friend, Henry Cabot Lodge, "He never once indulged in the base language of the curse." [299] And according to his eldest son, "I never heard him utter a coarse or profane word–though he was often mad and unafraid to show it." [300]

Once, after soon arriving in the Dakota territories as a greenhorn cattleman, he confronted a cowboy with a bad habit of pouring forth a profusion of profanity. Bystanders began nervously moving away from the two–the man apparently had a reputation for a temper as foul as his mouth. He was wont to use his pistols at the slightest provocation. The rumor among the ranch hands was that he'd killed five men. Roosevelt was, as always, fearless. "A big man should never lower himself to small language," he told the renegade. He didn't flinch when the man fixed him with a ferociously threatening glare. But then, to everyone's amazement, the man dropped his eyes and admitted as much. "Perhaps you're right, Mr. Roosevelt," he sheepishly replied. "I'd best hold my tongue." Bill Sewell, a rough backwoods guide, later commented, "I've never seen anything like it. It was almost as if Roosevelt could just speak a word or two and wield a kind of moral command over everyone else around him." [301]

Thus, when others would resort to ribald expletives, Roosevelt would utter one of his famous substitutes. "Bully" was his favorite declaration. It expressed everything from joyous approval to enthusiastic surprise. "Bullfeathers" was another favorite assertion. Likewise, he often burst forth with "by Jove," "that's just dandy," "jolly good," "blast," "hup to," "shiver me timbers," "holy Toledo," and "goodness gracious.[302]

He believed that language, like leadership, was an expression of character. To debase language is the inevitable result of an already debased character. To act shamefully is simply to reveal an already shameful estate. To dishonor and defile the conscience of another with rudeness or crudeness is merely the exposure of a dishonored and defiled character.

For Roosevelt the responsibilities of leadership demanded positive clarity of expression–and excluded any possibility of crass abasement:

> *Before a man can discipline other men, he must demonstrate his ability to discipline himself. Before he may be allowed the command of commission, he must evidence command of character. Look then to the work of his hands. Hear the words of his mouth. By his fruit you shall know him.*[303]

FAITH

We stand at Armageddon and we battle for the Lord.[304]

Whatever Theodore Roosevelt believed, he believed it strongly. His opinions were stated with the certainty of a creed. His policies were draped in the sanctity of revelation. That is simply because he had a very carefully worked-out worldview; and his perspective of life was securely anchored to certain immutable articles of faith.

According to his own testimony, these articles of faith were defined by traditional Christian orthodoxy. "I am a Christian statesman," he often averred.[305] And thus, he was "unable to accept the Pagan view of the world–or even that of Humanism."[306] To his mind the Christian world view was a comprehensive frame of reference touching the totality of life, not simply the hazy zone of personal piety. Christianity was for him, not merely a plan of salvation, an ethical system, or an exercise in mysticism. It was truth. It was truth about all things for all men at all times.

Thus, he urged the American people to be ever vigilant in the maintenance of their faith. Indeed, he was fearful of any sort of lapse of authentic Christian expression among the citizenry:

> *No abounding of material prosperity shall avail*
> *us if our spiritual senses atrophy. The foes of*
> *our own household will surely prevail against*
> *us unless there be in our people an inner life*
> *which finds its outer expression in a morality*
> *like unto that preached by the seers and*
> *prophets of God when the grandeur that was*
> *Greece and the glory that was Rome still lay in*
> *the future.*[307]

Like so much else in his character and thought, his faith was inculcated early in his life by his beloved father:

> *Morning prayers were with my father. We used*
> *to stand at the foot of the stairs, and when*
> *father came down we called out, 'I speak for*
> *you and the cubby-hole too!' There were three*
> *of us young children, and we used to sit with*
> *father on the sofa while he conducted morning*
> *prayers. The place between father and the arm*
> *of the sofa we called the 'cubby-hole.' The child*
> *who got that place we regarded as especially*
> *favored both in comfort and somehow in rank*
> *and title.*[308]

He observed all the conventional exercises of his native Dutch Reformed background–and taught them to his children. He was always regular in attendance at church. And from about 1876 on, he taught a Sunday School class whenever the opportunity arose.

When questioned–as he often was by an inquisitive public–he was quick to state his system of doctrine was best summarized in the lyrics of his favorite hymn, *How Firm a Foundation*:

How firm a foundation, you saints of the Lord,
Is laid for your faith in his excellent Word!
What more can He say than to you He has said,
To you who for refuge to Jesus have fled?

Fear not, I am with you, O be not dismayed,
For I am your God, and will still give you aid.
I'll strengthen you, help you, and cause you to stand,
Upheld by My righteous, omnipotent hand.

When through the deep waters I call you to go,
The rivers of water shall not overflow.
For I will be with you, your troubles to bless,
And sanctify to you your deepest distress.

When through fiery trials your pathway shall lie,
My grace, all sufficient, shall be your supply.
The flame shall not hurt you; I only design,
Your dross to consume and your gold to refine.

E'en down to old age all my people shall prove,
My sovereign, eternal, unchangeable love.
And when hoary hair shall their temples adorn,
Like lambs they shall still in my bosom be born.

The soul that on Jesus has leaned for repose,
I will not, I will not desert to his foes.
That soul, though all hell should endeavor to shake,
I'll never, no never, no never forsake.[309]

Believing that all leadership is in the end moral leadership, Roosevelt was convinced that a leader's faith must be firmly established. Quite obviously, his was.

THE BIBLE

I try to avoid that species of intensely offensive spiritual pride which takes the form of sniggering conceit in being heterodox.[310]

*T*heodore Roosevelt stood foursquare on the legacy of Biblical orthodoxy. He often asserted that he was "proud of his Holland, Huguenot, and Covenanting ancestors, and proud that the blood of that stark Puritan divine Jonathan Edwards flows in the veins of my children." [311]

This strongly affirmed Reformed heritage centered on a determined reverence for the comprehensive authority of the Bible–in its applicability to both the spiritual life and material life. It was a fully integrated tradition that recognized the Bible's relevance to sociology as well as salvation, to reform as well as redemption, and to culture as well as conversion.

Thus, he made Bible reading and Bible study a vital part of his daily life–and he encouraged others to likewise partake of its great wisdom. "A thorough knowledge of the Bible," he argued, "is worth more than a college education." [312]

Again, the reason for this was not simply that the Bible outlined a good and acceptable system of personal morals and social etiquette. He believed that the Bible was far more than that—that it was, in fact, the very warp and woof of the fabric of western civilization. It was, therefore, an essential element of the maintenance of order, civility, and prosperity. Indeed, without it, the great American experiment in liberty would be thrown into very real jeopardy:

> *Every thinking man, when he thinks, realizes*
> *that the teachings of the Bible are so interwo-*
> *ven and entwined with our whole civic and*
> *social life that it would be literally impossible*
> *for us to figure ourselves what that life would*
> *be if these standards were removed. We would*
> *lose almost all the standards by which we now*
> *judge both public and private morals; all the*
> *standards which we, with more or less resolu-*
> *tion, strive to raise ourselves.*[313]

He quoted the Bible often—evincing his intimate familiarity with it. One biographical archivist examined his published works and found he so had integrated Scripture into his thought processes, that there were actually more than 4,200 Biblical images, references, inferences, or complete quotations contained therein. And his unpublished letters, articles, and speeches contained hundreds—perhaps even thousands—more.[314]

In 1902, during the height of an extremely tense diplomatic showdown with Britain and Germany over their forcible recovery of debt service in Venezuela, several key military advisors were summoned to the White House. When they entered Roosevelt's office they found him furiously poring over a well-worn Bible and an exhaustive concordance. After a long and uncomfortable silence during which the president never acknowledged their presence, one of the generals cleared his throat and addressed the great man, "You asked for us, sir?" Without looking up from the volumes before him the president responded, "Well, don't just stand there men. I need help. I can't remember why I hold to the Monroe Doctrine. I know that it's got to be in here somewhere." Still not quite comprehending what he wanted them to do, the men moved toward his desk, whereupon the president handed each of them a Bible to peruse. "Get to work, men," he told them. "I can't act without warrant. I can't pronounce policy without precedence or precept." [315]

Roosevelt believed that there were absolutes. To his mind true leadership must always be accountable to that set of unchanging principles–ones not affected by the movement of the clock or the advance of the calendar. And he believed that those absolute principles could only reliably be found in the Book of Books–the Bible.

THE CHURCH

*A churchless society is most assuredly a society on
the downgrade.*[316]

*R*oosevelt was an enthusiastic churchman. He grew
up in the church, raised his children in the church,
and remained in the church until his dying day. He did not
"think much of a religion so internalized and subjective that
it found no expression in outward corporate worship."[317] His
reasoning was simple and straightforward: "Man was made
for covenant."[318]

His personal experience with the church was a happy
one–and he drew great strength from it. As he confessed to
his friends, "After a week of wrestling with perplexing problems, it does so rest my soul to come into the house of the
Lord and to sing–and to mean it–Holy, Holy, Holy, Lord God
Almighty."[319]

In ordinary times, in times of crisis, and in times of
ecstasy and joy, Roosevelt found himself most comfortable in
the midst of the fellowship of faith. It was there that he was
refreshed in his charge to defend the values, virtues, and

vision that had made America the last great bastion of Christian civilization:

> *There are those who believe that a new moder-*
> *nity demands a new morality. What they fail to*
> *consider is the harsh reality that there is no*
> *such thing as a new morality. There is only one*
> *morality. All else is immorality. There is only*
> *true Christian ethics over against which stands*
> *the whole of paganism. If we are to fulfill our*
> *great destiny as a people, then we must return*
> *to the old morality, the sole morality. And if we*
> *are to do that, then the church must prepare us*
> *for such a task.*[320]

But, even apart from these essentially spiritual and covenantal concerns, Roosevelt believed that the institutional church played an essential function in American society and culture. His study of history had convinced him that without the active interplay of its salt and light, communities inevitably began to decay:

> *In the pioneer days of the West we found it an*
> *unfailing rule that after a community had*
> *existed for a certain length of time either a*
> *church was built or else the community began*
> *to go down hill. In those old communities in*
> *the Eastern States which have gone backward,*
> *it is noticeable that the retrogression has been*
> *both marked by and accentuated by a rapid*
> *decline in church membership and work; the*
> *two facts being so interrelated that each stands*
> *to the other partly as a cause and partly as an*
> *effect.*[321]

Though he was a bit of a free-thinker when it came to theological issues—at times advocating rather marginal positions on key points of dogma—he was not favorably disposed toward liberal or neo-orthodox theology. Chief among the reasons was that such theology seemed to undermine the stability of a congregation's ongoing mission in the community and the world. Thus, he was an outspoken advocate for tradition—both in practice and belief. He even strove to honor the injunction to "keep the Sabbath." He always refrained from hunting, fishing, playing games, or transacting any sort of business on Sunday.

In addition, he was active as a witness to his faith, regularly inviting his friends to attend church with him. When John Willis—who had initiated him into the rough and tumble ways of frontier living—claimed to have made a man of him, Roosevelt replied, "Yes, John made a man out of me, but I made a Christian out of John. I actually had to drag him kicking and screaming in to the church house the first few times." [322]

When his eldest child Alice became a teenager, she went through a difficult period of rebellion. In particular, she had decided that church was just "humbug." One Sunday morning at Sagamore Hill she simply refused to dress and prepare herself for the morning worship services. Roosevelt told her in no uncertain terms that he would not tolerate "infidels" in his home. [323]

He recognized that by the very nature of his task as a parent, he had to impose his will upon his children at times. That is actually the essence of leadership: to move people in a direction that they would not ordinarily go of their own accord—but in which they must go, if they are to attain to their own peculiar calling.

Alice went to church that morning—and every Sunday afterward.

TR AND FDR

*Woe to the man or to the nation that stands as once
Laodicea stood; as the people of ancient Meroz
stood, when they dared not come to the help of the
Lord against the mighty.*[324]

*T*here are two figures that dominated the American
scene in the twentieth century. The first was
Theodore Roosevelt. The second, remarkably, was his young
cousin, Franklin Roosevelt. Both men possessed great personal
charisma, keen political instincts, penetrating social con-
sciences, seemingly boundless energy, and brilliantly diverse
intellects. Both of them left a lasting impress upon the world.
But that is where the similarity between the two ends. In every
other way, they could not have been more different.[325]

Franklin Roosevelt was the patriarch of the Hyde Park
side of the family. A Harvard-educated lawyer, he began his
political career as a Democratic party reformer in the New
York State Senate. His vigorous campaign on behalf of
Woodrow Wilson–against his famous cousin–during the 1912
presidential election earned him an appointment as assistant

secretary of the Navy. In 1920, he was the vice presidential running mate on the losing Democratic ticket. Eight years later, after a crippling bout with polio, he was elected to the first of two terms as New York's governor. Finally, in 1932, he ran for the presidency against the Depression-plagued Herbert Hoover and won overwhelmingly. During his record four terms, he directed the ambitious transformation of American government, created the modern system of social welfare, guided the nation through World War II, and laid the foundations for the United Nations.

Theodore Roosevelt was a conservative social reformer who wanted to firmly and faithfully reestablish the "Old World Order." [326] Franklin Roosevelt, on the other hand, was a liberal social revolutionary who wanted to boldly and unashamedly usher in the "New World Order." [327]

Theodore Roosevelt's motto was "speak softly and carry a big stick." [328] Franklin Roosevelt's motto was "good neighbors live in solidarity." [329]

Theodore Roosevelt spoke forcefully, but led the world into a remarkable epoch of peace–he even won the Nobel Peace Prize in 1905. Like his mentor, Woodrow Wilson, Franklin Roosevelt spoke of peace, but led the world into the bloodiest confrontation in man's tortured history.

The difference between the two perspectives was fundamental and presuppositional. Whereas Franklin Roosevelt's liberal global vision was informed by an unhesitatingly humanistic worldview, Theodore Roosevelt's conservative civic vision was informed by an uncompromising Christian worldview. In fact, while Franklin Roosevelt rejected the faith of his fathers early in his life, Theodore Roosevelt held tenaciously to the spiritual legacy that had been passed on to him by his father and grandfather. He often reveled in his Dutch Reformed and Scottish Covenanter roots. And the family ties to "that stark Puritan divine Jonathan Edwards" was for him a point of special pride.[330]

The practical outworking of these two models for American life and culture was dramatic: Franklin Roosevelt's led to invasive bureaucracy at home and intrusive adventurism abroad, while Theodore Roosevelt's led to progressive grassroots reform at home and sagacious cooperation abroad. Franklin Roosevelt's vision paved the way for modern liberalism, accomodationism, federal interventionism, and the New Left. Theodore Roosevelt's vision paved the way for modern conservatism, anti-communism, communitarian responsibility, and the New Right.

Both men understood the very critical notion that ideas have consequences. As a result, the twentieth century in America has largely been the tale of two households–of the Roosevelts of Sagamore Hill and of the Roosevelts of Hyde Park.

SAGAMORE HILL

At Sagamore Hill we love a great many things–birds and trees and books and all things beautiful, children and gardens and hard work and the joy of life.[331]

*L*ike Ulysses, Theodore Roosevelt had seen all the wonder of the world. He traveled extensively throughout North America, Europe, Africa, the Middle East, and Central and South America. He enjoyed his stays amidst the hustle and bustle of the world's greatest cities. And he relished his opportunities to tramp about in the world's most untamed wildernesses. But his lifelong conviction was that for all the majesty, splendor, mystery of those distant realms, there was no place like home.

Home for him was Sagamore Hill. It was the home he had designed and built overlooking Oyster Bay on Long Island. It was a spacious, old-fashioned house surrounded by wide porches and punctuated with a bevy of large fireplaces. Its shingled exterior was notable for its profusion of gables and chimneys, while the interior boasted large rooms with high ceilings, dark Edwardian furnishings, and dozens of hunting trophies in every available nook and cranny.

In every way the house reflected the personality of the larger-than-life family which occupied it. Jacob Riis testified that it "fairly shouted the vim, vigor, and vitality of its proprietors." [332]

Through the years the house served as a Mecca for the distinguished men of the age. It was the meeting place for all those whose ideas, actions, and intentions animated the time with optimism and confidence. Scientists, naturalists, thinkers, writers, artists, statesmen, reformers, and businessmen gathered there to imbibe of the atmosphere and to sit in the proximity of their greatest champion and mentor.

It was there at Sagamore Hill that the military strategy for the Spanish American War was hammered out. It was there that the Progressive movement was birthed. It was there that the determination to build the Panama Canal was confirmed. And it was there that the "carry a big stick" policy was first conceived.

But as much as the home served as the hub of national and international activity, it was also Roosevelt's refuge from the cares of the world. Until he became president he refused to have a phone installed in the place. The house was his getaway, his refuge, and his solace.

Originally sitting on more than a hundred acres, the property was a haven of rest for him. He could think there. He could rest there. He could enjoy his children–and later, his grandchildren–there. And he could enjoy his beloved outdoors there. He considered it "the one place on earth where the affairs of this poor fallen world very nearly seem to be set aright." [333]

Often, Roosevelt would spend hours sitting on the front porch simply rocking. Of course, for him, simply rocking took on a whole new definition: he rocked his chair so vigorously that it would traverse the entire length of the porch. Edith often scolded him for his hyperactivity. He just replied, "You relax your way, I'll relax mine." [334]

At the end of his life, he took special comfort in his home. Tired from his many battles, enfeebled by his injuries and illnesses, and frustrated by the foolhardiness of the Wilson administration's handling of vital issues of national interest, Roosevelt often retreated to his library and porches to think, reflect, convalesce, and rest.

The night he died, his final words to Edith were, "I wonder if you will ever know how I love Sagamore Hill." [335]

He knew better than most that leaders must have a sanctuary in which to retreat. There is, indeed, no place like home.

AMERICAN SPIRIT

In the fight for Americanism there must be no sag-ging back.[336]

*T*heodore Roosevelt's seemingly compulsive busyness was not mere hyperactivity. Nor was it the fruit of some primordial workaholism. Instead, labor was the natural product of what he called "the strenuous life." [337] For him, it was both a philosophy of life and a sense of mission:

I always believe in going hard at everything. My experience is that it pays never to let up or grow slack and fall behind.[338]

Once, Jacob Riis visited Roosevelt at the governor's residence in Albany. He was taken to the basement where the great man was getting a shave and a haircut. In order to keep busy, he was straddling a lap desk across his knees so that he could catch up on his correspondence. Simultaneously, he had three secretaries arrayed around him to whom he was dictating in alternating paragraphs. To one he was composing the final chapters of his biography of Oliver Cromwell; to another he was outlining portions of his upcoming legislative agenda; and to the third he was drafting a speech he would give later in the afternoon. All while writing on his lap and receiving a shave and a haircut! Riis could hardly believe his eyes. Riis asked him how he could possibly do so much at once. Roosevelt shrugged and responded that he was simply trying "to make the most of the time." [339]

For him, the injunction to "make the most of every opportunity" was a non-negotiable imperative predicated not on his abilities and gifts, but on his calling and faithfulness. [340] His whole life was lived according to the dictate, "Get action! Don't flinch! Don't foul! Hit the line hard!" [341] In fact, he believed that his many accomplishments were attributable to his early apprehension of this principle rather than any innate propensity to greatness that he may have inherited or inculcated.

This was in fact, his understanding of the special American spirit. It was a kind of national exceptionalism rooted in vision, effort, and valor:

> *America has not attained to greatness because*
> *of what we are or what we have. We have*
> *become the exemplars of all the world because*
> *of what we have done with what we are and*
> *what we have.* [342]

He believed that kind of achievement brought with it a certain responsibility–one that could not be shirked but at great hazard to all:

> *Our place must be great among the nations. We*
> *may either fail greatly or succeed greatly; but*
> *we cannot avoid the endeavor from which*

> *either great failure or great success must come.*
> *Even if we would, we cannot play a small part.*
> *If we should try, all that would follow would*
> *be that we should play a large part ignobly.*[343]

Some called his attitude jingoism, others patriotism, and still others simply enthusiasm. But for Roosevelt, his conception of American nationalism was the capstone of his whole philosophy of life:

> *America was not born of a single people or a*
> *single tradition or a single movement. Rather,*
> *our nation was born of a single idea–one that*
> *transcends the mere material attachments of*
> *other ethnicities. Our nation was born of the*
> *peculiar notion that all men were born to be*
> *free. Thus, America is the best expression of the*
> *highest aspiration of mankind. Best we safe-*
> *guard such a sacred trust for all other nations*
> *with all the fervor and ardor we can muster.*
> *Therein lies the American spirit.*[344]

All his ebullience for American ingenuity, all his enthusiasm for American achievement, and all his exuberance for American valor was merely an expression of this idea: that with great privileges come great responsibilities, that blessings bring with them duties, and that the joy of liberty is the most sober obligation ever entrusted to men or nations.

PART III:
THE LEGACY OF THEODORE ROOSEVELT

"The world is at this moment passing through one of those terrible periods of convulsion when the souls of men and of nations are tried as by fire. Woe to the man or to the nation that at such a time stands as once Laodicea stood; as the people of ancient Meroz stood, when they dared not come to the help of the Lord against the mighty. In such a crisis the moral weakling is the enemy of the right, the enemy of life, liberty, and the pursuit of happiness."[345]

THE MICAH MANDATE

The most dangerous form of sentimental debauch is to give expression to good wishes on behalf of virtue while you do nothing about it. Justice is not merely words. It is to be translated into acts.[346]

*I*n 1917, when American troops were preparing to sail across the seas in order to take to the battlefields of France and Belgium in the First World War, the New York Bible Society asked Roosevelt to inscribe a message in the pocket New Testaments that each of the soldiers would be given. The great man happily complied. And he began by quoting a striking Biblical call for a life of balance–what he called the "Micah Mandate." [347]

He has shown you, O man, what is good and what the Lord requires of you: but to do justice, and to love mercy, and to walk humbly with your God. (Micah 6:8)

Saying that, "The whole teaching of the New Testament" is actually "foreshadowed in Micah's verse," Roosevelt exhorted the men to lead the world in "both word and deed" through unimpeachable moral uprightness.[348]

In his brief message to the soldiers, he explained:

> *Do justice; and therefore fight valiantly against those that stand for the reign of Moloch and Beelzebub on this earth. Love mercy; treat your enemies well; succor the afflicted; treat every woman as if she were your sister; care for the little children; and be tender with the old and helpless. Walk humbly; you will do so if you study the life and teachings of the Savior, walking in His steps.*[349]

He concluded, saying:

> *Remember: the most perfect machinery of government will not keep us as a nation from destruction if there is not within us a soul. No abounding of material prosperity shall avail us if our spiritual senses atrophy. The foes of our own household will surely prevail against us unless there be in our people an inner life which finds its outward expression in a morality like unto that preached by the seers and prophets of God when the grandeur that was Greece and the glory that was Rome still lay in the future.*[350]

Roosevelt believed that the ultimate security of men and nations depended on a faithful adherence to the venerable Old Testament prophet's three-fold demonstration of moral and practical balance: a strident commitment to justice, a tangible concern for mercy, and a reverent humility before the Almighty. He was certain that even with the deployment of superior forces in superior numbers with superior armaments, the American armies would ultimately be defeated during the war–if they took to the field bereft of this kind of personal integrity. And he was convinced that if individuals and families took only their limited material resources into the conflagration of our daily warfare, they too would be defeated and destroyed.

In his own life, these beacon lights of justice, mercy, and humility continually guided his steps–and they provide for us a key to understanding his great effectiveness as a leader.

JUSTICE

*F*or Roosevelt the idea of justice was inextricably linked with the principle of righteousness. They were inseparable concepts as far as he was concerned. In both his public pronouncements and his private predilections, he made it plain that any attempt to secure justice, whether at home, in the community, or among the nations–any attempt, apart from the clearly revealed ethical parameters of goodness, truth, purity, and faithfulness–would surely prove to be utter folly. On the other hand, he believed just as emphatically that any people that diligently sought to do right–to do righteousness–would inevitably pursue justice as well.

According to his very tightly conceived worldview, the two simply went together. One could not be had without the other.

Again and again he sounded the refrain:

> *A true patriot must necessarily be a zealot and fighter for the truth. He must hold to the mean and enforce the dictates of righteousness with justice.*[351]

*Righteousness and justice flow on like a river–
this then is the high call of freedom.*[352]

*The golden middle course of liberty is held by
the crusader for truth with the sword of righteousness in one hand and the trowel of justice
in the other.*[353]

Roosevelt was thoroughly convinced that there could be
no standard for the outward life if there were no standard for
the inward life. But, simultaneously, there could be no inward
standard if there were no outward standard. For him, justice
and righteousness were completely inseparable.

Gouverneur Morris was one of Roosevelt's heroes; the
biography he wrote of the great merchant, lawyer, and planter
from Pennsylvania was one of his earliest literary and historical triumphs. Morris–who was actually responsible for the
draft version of the Constitution–believed, with Alexander
Hamilton, Patrick Henry, George Washington, and many of
the other framers, that in order for the American experiment
in liberty to succeed, justice and righteousness had to be
"welded together as one in the hearts and minds of the citizenry."[354] Thus, he said:

*Liberty and justice simply cannot be had apart
from the gracious influences of a righteous people. A righteous people simply cannot exist
apart from the aspiration to liberty and justice.
The Christian religion and its incumbent
morality is tied to the cause of freedom with a
Gordian knot; loose one from the other and
both are sent asunder.*[355]

The influence of Morris on Roosevelt was, quite understandably, great. So, according to his conception, good citizenship and personal virtue were essential aspects of the same bolt of fabric. He could tolerate no distinction between the inward and outward, the heart and the hand, the soul and the body–thus his affinity for the "Micah Mandate."

> *He has shown you, O man, what is good and*
> *what the Lord requires of you: but to do justice,*
> *and to love mercy, and to walk humbly with*
> *your God. (Micah 6:8)*

MERCY

*I*n the same way that Roosevelt associated justice with the practice of righteousness, he linked mercy with the exercise of authority. They too were inseparable concepts in his carefully worked out scheme. He did not believe that authority could be had apart from mercy–and vice versa.

He was unflinching in his declaration: if anyone were ever to influence their families or their culture to stand for goodness, faithfulness, and kindness, then they would have to graciously serve the hurts, wants, and needs all around them:

> *The greatest men are those who would willingly serve in the shadows. The least and the last are the first and the foremost.*[356]

> *We must strive, each of us, so as to conduct our own lives as to be, to a certain extent at least, our brother's keeper.*[357]

> *A life of authentic concern for the less privileged is the badge of authority in a culture. Acts of mercy are the only credentials for true greatness.*[358]

This is one of the most basic principles of the leadership: the ability to lead a society is earned not inherited. And it is earned through faithful, compassionate, and merciful service. Unfortunately, this principle has not been widely understood by most modern men and women-even by those of us who have been thrust into roles of grave responsibility.

In fact, the whole concept of servanthood-the high calling to exercise mercy-is a much neglected, largely forgotten vocation today. As a result, many of the gains and many of the distinctives of our culture have been needlessly eroded.

This is, after all, one of the greatest legacies the scions of Western Civilization have passed on to us. It was the spirit of merciful service in the West that launched the first hospitals, orphanages, almshouses, soup kitchens, charitable societies, relief agencies, rescue missions, hostels, and shelters. And, as a result, that commitment to cooperation, accountability, and responsibility led Western civilization to new heights of freedom and prosperity for nearly two millennium.

Call it what you will-silk-stocking idealism, high-handed philanthropy, *noblesse oblige*, covenantal chivalry, or the square deal-Roosevelt was firmly convinced that mercy was an indispensable public and private virtue.

> *He has shown you, O man, what is good and what the Lord requires of you: but to do justice, and to love mercy, and to walk humbly with your God. (Micah 6:8)*

HUMILITY

*T*he traditional Christian approach to any issue, or any problem, or any situation, or any circumstance–in fact, the traditional Christian approach to the whole of life–has always been theocentric. In other words, it begins and ends with, and is ultimately centered in, the Lord God Himself. He is, after all, the Alpha and the Omega of all things in reality. Thus, for the orthodox to attempt any approach to reality without this in view is to invite frustration and failure. God is sovereign. This is the fundamental truth that underlies the whole of the Christian worldview–from epistemology to soteriology. It comes as no surprise then that Roosevelt believed that a good man or woman's life should be entirely suffused with a holy fear and reverence of Him–to the point that everything else is thereby affected:

> *If fear of the Almighty is the beginning of wisdom, then surely fear of the Almighty is the starting place of any fruitful endeavor.*[359]

> *It is a humbling matter to consider the wide gulf, the gaping chasm that exists in this poor*

> *sin-besotted world between creature and*
> *Creator.*[360]

> *Tremble in His midst so as to never falter in the*
> *midst of the grave responsibilities of life.*
> *Humility properly placed is the only sure foun-*
> *dation of leadership.*[361]

Humility is not exactly a popular concept these days. Fernanda Eberstadt, in her brilliant coming-of-age novel *Isaac and His Devils*, captured the prevailing sentiment of our time:

> *Humility has a dank and shameful smell to the*
> *worldly, the scent of failure, lowliness, and*
> *obscurity.*[362]

But of course, such has not always been the case. In times past, humility was considered to be a virtue of supreme value. Applying this most fundamental truth to the arena of national and cultural integrity, George Washington asserted:

> *It is the first duty of all nations to acknowledge*
> *the providence of Almighty God, to obey His*
> *will, to be grateful for His benefits, and to*
> *humbly implore His protection and favor in*
> *holy fear.*[363]

Roosevelt believed that, likewise, it was the first duty of all men and women.

> *He has shown you, O man, what is good and*
> *what the Lord requires of you: but to do justice,*
> *and to love mercy, and to walk humbly with*
> *your God. (Micah 6:8)*

OUR NEED

*A*t a vast memorial meeting in Philadelphia following the sudden and grievous death of Theodore Roosevelt, Senator George Wharton Pepper summarized the import of the great man's legacy–his unflinching legacy of justice, mercy, and humility–to future generations:

> *We as a people have sore need of Theodore*
> *Roosevelt. But not only collectively do we need*
> *him. We need him as individuals. When we*
> *look into our hearts we find that we shall have*
> *sustained a personal loss if we allow the*
> *Colonel to leave us. You and I need him as a*
> *factor in our daily lives. We have more energy*
> *when the Colonel is about. We are less content*
> *to submit to injustice, less appalled by obsta-*
> *cles in the path of progress. With the Colonel*
> *near we are far braver men and finer women.*
> *Where the Colonel leads we are sure of the*
> *direction in which we are moving. When he*
> *gives commands we are not in doubt about our*

objective. Happily, it will not be difficult to keep him with us. Theodore Roosevelt alive is easy to conceive of; Theodore Roosevelt dead is altogether unthinkable. Such a man strengthens our belief in immortality. He has but gone to that front from which nobody would dare to hold him back.[364]

He continued his eloquent eulogy, saying:

The immortality of personal influence is God's greatest gift to man. When conscience cowers, when advice proves powerless, when reason plays me false, his influence makes a man of me. I cannot cheat while he is in the game. I cannot drift when he is headed upstream. I cannot talk nonsense when he is there to hear. Dead? No. Today we are rejoicing because Theodore Roosevelt is more alive than ever. There is not a tinge of sadness in our celebration. The immortality of his influence makes us glad with an exceeding great joy.[365]

Finally, he concluded by quoting the great man himself:

Just beyond man's narrow daily vision stand the immortals. And Jehovah opened the eyes of the young man, and he saw; and behold, the mountain was full of horses and chariots of fire about Elisha. At the front of this nation's way ride the strong guards of our own past, their authority immortalized by death. In the hour of decision we see them; their grave eyes watch us,

the keepers of our standards, the builders of our
freedom. They came from God to do His bid-
ding—and returned. To each of them the past
has given his own labor. The future we cannot
see; nor what the next imperious task; nor who
its strong executant. But for this generation the
task is clear: you who gird yourselves for this
great fight in the never-ending warfare for the
good of mankind, we stand at Armageddon and
we battle for the Lord.[366]

THE LESSONS OF LEADERSHIP

"The hardest lessons to learn are those that are the most obvious."[367]

↝ The first prerequisite of true leadership is a happy home. The private life is the proving ground for the public life.

↝ Leadership must be modeled on some tangible, practical, and realizable ideal. Leaders have mentors. They are disciples. They comprehend the notion of legacy.

↝ Leaders are those who make the most of every moment, every opportunity, and every available resource.

↝ Leadership is the art of pursuing the ideal in the midst of a world that is something less than ideal.

↝ If you want to lead, you must read.

↝ A leader cannot lead a nation if he can not vividly portray the path which he wishes to take.

↝ True leadership is a life committed to good deeds.

↝ A leader's goal, first and foremost, is to reach the goal.

↝ A leader is an idealist who is simultaneously blessed with a strong dose of reality.

↝ The role of the leader is primarily to serve as a moral compass—pointing others toward the true north of justice and righteousness.

↝ A leader knows that what is really important in life rarely puts on airs of importance.

↝ There is little extraordinary about the achievements of a genius, a prodigy, or a savant. Inevitably, a great leader is someone who overcomes tremendous obstacles and still succeeds.

꙾ The essence of leadership is the ability to maintain great strength without any impulsive compulsion to use it. That strength is to be held in reserve, until and unless it becomes necessary to use it for the cause of right.

꙾ A wise leader always uses whatever resources are placed at his disposal–but he never confuses the means with the ends.

꙾ A leader will always attempt to unite others' disparate and distinctive legacies–and in so doing, help begin the vital process of healing.

꙾ A leader has the ability to take any circumstance and see it through the lens of happy providence. He is living proof of the fact that laughter is indeed the best medicine.

꙾ The efficacy of leadership depends, to a large degree, on the leader's incognizance of the negative consequences of doing right.

꙾ A leader understands that failure is the backdoor to success.

꙾ A leader is able to maintain a wide circle of relationships through a generous application of the social graces, but simultaneously guards his private affairs–maintaining genuine intimacy only with those whom he can trust implicitly.

꙾ No commendation is greater than the condemnation of one's fiercest sworn enemies.

꙾ Social movements need far more than a gifted or popular leader. They need a consensus wrought by a common worldview and a common faith.

꙾ A leader will always prefer to be faithful than famous.

꙾ A leader invariably lives his life as a sincere imitator of the best attributes of others. Heroes always have heroes.

꙾ The responsibilities of leadership demand positive clarity of expression–and exclude any possibility of crass abasement.

꙾ Because all leadership is in the end moral leadership, a leader's faith must be firmly established.

꙾ True leadership must always be accountable to that set of unchanging principles–ones that are not affected by the movement of the clock or the advance of the calendar.

∞ The essence of leadership is to move people in a direction that they would not ordinarily go of their own accord—but in which they must go if they are to attain to their own peculiar calling.

∞ Great leaders understand the very critical notion that ideas have consequences.

∞ Leaders must have a sanctuary in which to retreat. There is indeed no place like home.

∞ With great privileges come great responsibilities. Blessings bring with them duties. And the joy of liberty is the most sober obligation ever entrusted to men or nations.

BIBLIOGRAPHY

"Books are the greatest of companions."[368]

Books by Theodore Roosevelt

1882	*The Naval War of 1812*
1885	*Hunting Trips of a Ranchman*
1887	*Thomas Hart Benton*
1888	*Essays on Practical Politics*
1888	*Gouverneur Morris*
1888	*Ranch Life and the Hunting Trail*
1889	*The Winning of the West*, vols. 1-2
1891	*New York*
1893	*The Wilderness Hunter*
1893	*American Big Game*, with George Bird Grinnell
1894	*The Winning of the West*, vol. 3
1895	*Hero Tales from American History*, with Henry Cabot Lodge
1895	*Hunting in Many Lands*, with George Bird Grinnell
1897	*American Ideals*
1897	*Some American Game*
1897	*Trail and Campfire*, with George Bird Grinnell
1899	*The Rough Riders*
1900	*Oliver Cromwell*
1900	*The Strenuous Life*
1902	*The Deer Family*, with T.S. Van Dyke, D.G. Elliot, and A.J. Stone

1904	*Addresses and Messages*
1905	*Outdoor Pastimes of an American Hunter*
1907	*Good Hunting*
1909	*Outlook Editorials*
1910	*African and European Addresses*
1910	*African Game Trails*
1910	*American Problems*
1910	*The New Nationalism*
1910	*Presidential Addresses and State Papers*, 8 vols.
1912	*The Conservation of Womanhood and Childhood*
1912	*Realizable Goals*
1913	*Autobiography*
1913	*History as Literature*
1913	*Progressive Principles*
1914	*Through the Brazilian Wilderness*
1914	*African Game Animals*, with Edmund Heller
1915	*America and the World War*
1916	*A Book-Lover's Holiday in the Open*
1916	*Fear God and Take Your Own Part*
1917	*The Foes of Our Own Household*
1917	*Social Justice and Popular Rule*
1917	*National Strength and International Duty*
1918	*The Great Adventure*

Bishop, Joseph Bucklin, ed. *Letters to His Children.* New York: Scribners, 1926.

Hagedorn, Hermann, ed. *The Memorial Edition of the Works of Theodore Roosevelt*, 24 vols. New York: Scribners, 1926.

Morrison, Elting, ed. *The Letters of Theodore Roosevelt*, 2 vols. Cambridge, MA: Harvard University, 1951.

Wills, James Austin. *The Letters and Speeches of Theodore Roosevelt.* New York: Billington and Sons, 1937.

Books about Theodore Roosevelt

Lord Charnwood. *Theodore Roosevelt.* Boston: Atlantic Monthly, 1923.

Collier, Peter. *The Roosevelts: An American Saga.* New York: Simon & Schuster, 1994.

Dallimore, James. *The Long Shadow.* New York: Allan and Digby, 1962.

Dyer, Thomas. *Theodore Roosevelt and the Idea of Race.* Baton Rouge, LA: Louisiana State University, 1980.

Fulton, Maurice, ed. *Roosevelt's Writings.* New York: Macmillan, 1922.

Hagedorn, Hermann. *Life of Theodore Roosevelt.* New York: Harper Brothers, 1918.

––– *The Roosevelt Family of Sagamore Hill.* New York: Macmillan, 1954.

Hewlitt, Jonathan. *The American Impact.* London: Caprice and Meadows, 1956.

Howland, Harold. *Theodore Roosevelt and His Times.* New Haven, CT: Yale University, 1921.

Jeffers, H. Paul. *Commissioner Roosevelt.* New York: John Wiley & Sons, 1994.

Johnson, David. *Theodore Roosevelt: American Monarch.* Philadelphia: American History Sources, 1981.

Lever, James. *The Roosevelt Mythos.* New York: Dorrit-Justin, 1923.

Lowe, Mark Hammond. *Roosevelt and War.* New York: Garamond, 1922.

Longworth, Alice Roosevelt. *Crowded Hours.* New York: Scribners, 1933.

Miller, Nathan. *Theodore Roosevelt: A Life.* New York: William Morrow, 1992.

Morris, Charles. *The Marvelous Career of Theodore Roosevelt.* New York: John Winston, 1910.

Morris, Edmund. *The Rise of Theodore Roosevelt.* New York: Coward, McCann, and Geoghegan, 1979.

Riis, Jacob. *Theodore Roosevelt the Citizen.* New York: Macmillan, 1904.

Robinson, Corinne Roosevelt. *My Brother: Theodore Roosevelt.* New York: Scribners, 1921.

Roosevelt, Archibald, ed. *Race, Riots, Reds, and Crime.* New York: Roosevelt Memorial Association, 1939.

Russell, Thomas, ed. *Life and Work of Theodore Roosevelt.* New York: L. H. Walter, 1919.

Thayer, William Roscoe. *Theodore Roosevelt.* New York: Houghton Mifflin, 1919.

Wagenknecht, Edward. *The Seven Worlds of Theodore Roosevelt.* New York: Longmans and Green, 1958.

Wilson, Dorothy Clarke. *Alice and Edith.* New York: Doubleday, 1989.

Wister, Owen. *Roosevelt: The Story of a Friendship.* New York: Macmillan, 1930.

ENDNOTES

1. Theodore Roosevelt, *Realizable Ideals*, (New York: Scribner's, 1919), pp. 615-616.
2. John Buchan, *Sidelights and Adventures*, (Edinburgh, UK: Ballantine Press, 1946), p. 22.
3. Theodore Roosevelt, *American Ideals*, (New York: Scribner's, 1901), p. 4.
4. Thomas Russell, ed., *Life and Work of Theodore Roosevelt*, (New York: L.H. Walter, 1919), p. 76.
5. Thomas Russell, ed., *Life and Work of Theodore Roosevelt*, (New York: L.H. Walter, 1919), p. 193.
6. Thomas Russell, ed., *Life and Work of Theodore Roosevelt*, (New York: L.H. Walter, 1919), p. 194.
7. Maurice Fulton, ed., *Roosevelt's Writings*, (New York: Macmillan, 1922), p. xiii.
8. Edward Wagenknecht, *The Seven Worlds of Theodore Roosevelt*, (New York: Longmans and Green, 1958), p. 6.
9. Edward Wagenknecht, *The Seven Worlds of Theodore Roosevelt*, (New York: Longmans and Green, 1958), p. 33.
10. Howard Gleeson, *William Jennings Bryan*, (New York: Ingles and Bryson, 1923), p. 127.
11. Harold Tribble Cole, *The Coming Terror: Life Before the Great War*, (New York: Languine Bros., Publishers, 1936), p. 21.
12. Harold Tribble Cole, *The Coming Terror: Life Before the Great War*, (New York: Languine Bros., Publishers, 1936), p. 21.
13. Harold Tribble Cole, *The Coming Terror: Life Before the Great War*, (New York: Languine Bros., Publishers, 1936), p. 21.
14. Harold Tribble Cole, *The Coming Terror: Life Before the Great War*, (New York: Languine Bros., Publishers, 1936), p. 23.
15. Hilaire Belloc, *The Biographer's Art: Excerpts from Belloc's Florid Pen*, (London: Catholic Union, 1956), p. 33.
16. Howard F. Pallin, ed., *Literary English and Scottish Sermons*, (London: Windus Etheridge, 1937), p. 101.
17. E. Michael Jones, *Degenerate Moderns: Modernity as Rationalized Sexual Misbehavior*, (San Francisco: Ignatius Press, 1993), p. 9.
18. Theodore Roosevelt, *American Ideals*, (New York: Scribner's, 1901), p. 5.
19. Thomas Russell, ed., *Life and Work of Theodore Roosevelt*, (New York: L.H. Walter, 1919), p. 76.
20. Thomas Russell, ed., *Life and Work of Theodore Roosevelt*, (New York: L.H. Walter, 1919), p. 258.
21. Theodore Roosevelt, *Progressive Principles*, (New York: Scribner's, 1926), p. 22.
22. Thomas Russell, ed., *Life and Work of Theodore Roosevelt*, (New York: L.H. Walter, 1919), p. 240.
23. Thomas Russell, ed., *Life and Work of Theodore Roosevelt*, (New York: L.H. Walter, 1919), p. 240.
24. Thomas Russell, ed., *Life and Work of Theodore Roosevelt*, (New York: L.H. Walter, 1919), p. 240.
25. Thomas Russell, ed., *Life and Work of Theodore Roosevelt*, (New York: L.H. Walter, 1919), p. 240.
26. Nathan Miller, *Theodore Roosevelt*, (New York: William Morrow, 1992), p. 531.
27. Theodore Roosevelt, *Autobiography*, (New York: Scribners, 1924), p. 13.
28. Corinne Roosevelt Robinson, *My Brother Theodore Roosevelt*, (New York: Scribner's, 1921), p. 23.
29. Edmund Morris, *The Rise of Theodore Roosevelt*, (New York: Coward, McCann, & Geoghegan, 1979), p. 60.
30. Thomas Russell, ed., *Life and Work of Theodore Roosevelt*, (New York: L.H. Walter, 1919), p. 76.
31. Theodore Roosevelt, *Autobiography*, (New York: Scribners, 1924), p. 14.
32. Edmund Morris, *The Rise of Theodore Roosevelt*, (New York: Coward, McCann, & Geoghegan, 1979), p. 48.
33. Thomas Russell, ed., *Life and Work of Theodore Roosevelt*, (New York: L.H. Walter, 1919), p. 29.
34. Theodore Roosevelt, *Autobiography*, (New York: Scribners, 1924), p. 22.
35. Nathan Miller, *Theodore Roosevelt*, (New York: William Morrow, 1992), p. 64.

36. Nathan Miller, *Theodore Roosevelt*, (New York: William Morrow, 1992), p. 69.
37. Nathan Miller, *Theodore Roosevelt*, (New York: William Morrow, 1992), p. 69.
38. Thomas Russell, ed., *Life and Work of Theodore Roosevelt*, (New York: L.H. Walter, 1919), p. 191.
39. Thomas Russell, ed., *Life and Work of Theodore Roosevelt*, (New York: L.H. Walter, 1919), p. 192.
40. James Austin Wills, *The Letters and Speeches of Theodore Roosevelt*, (New York: Billington and Sons, 1937), p. 86.
41. Edmund Morris, *The Rise of Theodore Roosevelt*, (New York: Coward, McCann, & Geoghegan, 1979), p. 50.
42. Nathan Miller, *Theodore Roosevelt*, (New York: William Morrow, 1992), p. 87.
43. Nathan Miller, *Theodore Roosevelt*, (New York: William Morrow, 1992), p. 90.
44. Nathan Miller, *Theodore Roosevelt*, (New York: William Morrow, 1992), p. 101.
45. Edmund Morris, *The Rise of Theodore Roosevelt*, (New York: Coward, McCann, & Geoghegan, 1979), p. 136.
46. Edmund Morris, *The Rise of Theodore Roosevelt*, (New York: Coward, McCann, & Geoghegan, 1979), p. 135.
47. James Austin Wills, *The Letters and Speeches of Theodore Roosevelt*, (New York: Billington and Sons, 1937), p. 200.
48. Thomas Russell, ed., *Life and Work of Theodore Roosevelt*, (New York: L.H. Walter, 1919), p. 88.
49. James Austin Wills, *The Letters and Speeches of Theodore Roosevelt*, (New York: Billington and Sons, 1937), p. 86.
50. Nathan Miller, *Theodore Roosevelt*, (New York: William Morrow, 1992), p. 119.
51. Nathan Miller, *Theodore Roosevelt*, (New York: William Morrow, 1992), p. 122.
52. Thomas Russell, ed., *Life and Work of Theodore Roosevelt*, (New York: L.H. Walter, 1919), p. 197.
53. Thomas Russell, ed., *Life and Work of Theodore Roosevelt*, (New York: L.H. Walter, 1919), p. 198.
54. Nathan Miller, *Theodore Roosevelt*, (New York: William Morrow, 1992), p. 142.
55. James Austin Wills, *The Letters and Speeches of Theodore Roosevelt*, (New York: Billington and Sons, 1937), p. 55.
56. Nathan Miller, *Theodore Roosevelt*, (New York: William Morrow, 1992), p. 149.
57. Nathan Miller, *Theodore Roosevelt*, (New York: William Morrow, 1992), p. 109.
58. Nathan Miller, *Theodore Roosevelt*, (New York: William Morrow, 1992), p. 155.
59. Nathan Miller, *Theodore Roosevelt*, (New York: William Morrow, 1992), p. 155.
60. Thomas Russell, ed., *Life and Work of Theodore Roosevelt*, (New York: L.H. Walter, 1919), p. 214.
61. Thomas Russell, ed., *Life and Work of Theodore Roosevelt*, (New York: L.H. Walter, 1919), p. 116.
62. Nathan Miller, *Theodore Roosevelt*, (New York: William Morrow, 1992), pp. 163-164.
63. Edmund Morris, *The Rise of Theodore Roosevelt*, (New York: Coward, McCann, & Geoghegan, 1979), p. 298.
64. Thomas Russell, ed., *Life and Work of Theodore Roosevelt*, (New York: L.H. Walter, 1919), p. 116.
65. James Austin Wills, *The Letters and Speeches of Theodore Roosevelt*, (New York: Billington and Sons, 1937), p. 44.
66. Edmund Morris, *The Rise of Theodore Roosevelt*, (New York: Coward, McCann, & Geoghegan, 1979), p. 303.
67. Edmund Morris, *The Rise of Theodore Roosevelt*, (New York: Coward, McCann, & Geoghegan, 1979), p. 303.
68. Edmund Morris, *The Rise of Theodore Roosevelt*, (New York: Coward, McCann, & Geoghegan, 1979), p. 303.
69. Nathan Miller, *Theodore Roosevelt*, (New York: William Morrow, 1992), p. 184.
70. Thomas Russell, ed., *Life and Work of Theodore Roosevelt*, (New York: L.H. Walter, 1919), p. 132.
71. Nathan Miller, *Theodore Roosevelt*, (New York: William Morrow, 1992), p. 198.
72. Thomas Russell, ed., *Life and Work of Theodore Roosevelt*, (New York: L.H. Walter, 1919), p. 134.
73. Thomas Russell, ed., *Life and Work of Theodore Roosevelt*, (New York: L.H. Walter, 1919), p. 135.
74. Thomas Russell, ed., *Life and Work of Theodore Roosevelt*, (New York: L.H. Walter, 1919), p. 302.
75. Thomas Russell, ed., *Life and Work of Theodore Roosevelt*, (New York: L.H. Walter, 1919), p. 152.
76. Mark Hammond Lowe, *Roosevelt and War*, (New York: Garamond, 1922), p. 57.
77. Nathan Miller, *Theodore Roosevelt*, (New York: William Morrow, 1992), p. 274.
78. Mark Hammond Lowe, *Roosevelt and War*, (New York: Garamond, 1922), p. 235.
79. Theodore Roosevelt, *Autobiography*, (New York: Scribners, 1924), p. 355.
80. Maurice Fulton, ed., *Roosevelt's Writings*, (New York: Macmillan, 1922), p. 141.
81. Thomas Russell, ed., *Life and Work of Theodore Roosevelt*, (New York: L.H. Walter, 1919), p. 391.
82. Nathan Miller, *Theodore Roosevelt*, (New York: William Morrow, 1992), p. 346.
83. Nathan Miller, *Theodore Roosevelt*, (New York: William Morrow, 1992), p. 352.
84. James Austin Wills, *The Letters and Speeches of Theodore Roosevelt*, (New York: Billington and Sons, 1937), p. vii.

85. Maurice Fulton, ed., *Roosevelt's Writings*, (New York: Macmillan, 1922), p. 142.
86. Nathan Miller, *Theodore Roosevelt*, (New York: William Morrow, 1992), p. 381.
87. Thomas Russell, ed., *Life and Work of Theodore Roosevelt*, (New York: L.H. Walter, 1919), p. 341.
88. Nathan Miller, *Theodore Roosevelt*, (New York: William Morrow, 1992), p. 436.
89. Thomas Russell, ed., *Life and Work of Theodore Roosevelt*, (New York: L.H. Walter, 1919), p. 360.
90. Thomas Russell, ed., *The Political Battle of 1912*, (New York: L.H. Walter, 1912), p. 285.
91. Thomas Russell, ed., *The Political Battle of 1912*, (New York: L.H. Walter, 1912), p. 286.
92. Thomas Russell, ed., *The Political Battle of 1912*, (New York: L.H. Walter, 1912), p. 289.
93. Thomas Russell, ed., *The Political Battle of 1912*, (New York: L.H. Walter, 1912), p. 289.
94. Jonathan Hewlitt, *The American Impact*, (London: Caprice and Meadows, 1956), p. 184.
95. Thomas Russell, ed., *The Political Battle of 1912*, (New York: L.H. Walter, 1912), p. 2.
96. Woodrow Wilson, *The New Freedom*, (New York: Doubleday, Page, and Company, 1913), p. 3.
97. Woodrow Wilson, *The New Freedom*, (New York: Doubleday, Page, and Company, 1913), p. 3.
98. Woodrow Wilson, *The New Freedom*, (New York: Doubleday, Page, and Company, 1913), p. 7.
99. Woodrow Wilson, *The New Freedom*, (New York: Doubleday, Page, and Company, 1913), p. 4.
100. Woodrow Wilson, *The New Freedom*, (New York: Doubleday, Page, and Company, 1913), p. 4.
101. Woodrow Wilson, *The New Freedom*, (New York: Doubleday, Page, and Company, 1913), p. 35.
102. Woodrow Wilson, *The New Freedom*, (New York: Doubleday, Page, and Company, 1913), p. 50.
103. Woodrow Wilson, *The New Freedom*, (New York: Doubleday, Page, and Company, 1913), p. 14.
104. Jacob Riis, *Theodore Roosevelt: The Citizen*, (New York: Macmillan, 1904), p. 201.
105. Theodore Roosevelt, *Foes of Our Own Household*, (New York: Charles Scribner's Sons, 1917), p. 97.
106. Jacob Riis, *Theodore Roosevelt: The Citizen*, (New York: Macmillan, 1904), p. 285.
107. Thomas Russell, ed., *The Political Battle of 1912*, (New York: L.H. Walter, 1912), p. 204.
108. Thomas Russell, ed., *The Political Battle of 1912*, (New York: L.H. Walter, 1912), p. 205.
109. Thomas Russell, ed., *The Political Battle of 1912*, (New York: L.H. Walter, 1912), p. 93.
110. Jonathan Hewlitt, *The American Impact*, (London: Caprice and Meadows, 1956), p. 184.
111. Thomas Russell, ed., *Life and Work of Theodore Roosevelt*, (New York: L.H. Walter, 1919), p. 261.
112. Nathan Miller, *Theodore Roosevelt*, (New York: William Morrow, 1992), p. 261.
113. Nathan Miller, *Theodore Roosevelt*, (New York: William Morrow, 1992), p. 562.
114. Nathan Miller, *Theodore Roosevelt*, (New York: William Morrow, 1992), p. 562.
115. Thomas Russell, ed., *Life and Work of Theodore Roosevelt*, (New York: L.H. Walter, 1919), p. 341.
116. Nathan Miller, *Theodore Roosevelt*, (New York: William Morrow, 1992), p. 566.
117. Nathan Miller, *Theodore Roosevelt*, (New York: William Morrow, 1992), p. 566.
118. Nathan Miller, *Theodore Roosevelt*, (New York: William Morrow, 1992), p. 566.
119. James Austin Wills, *The Letters and Speeches of Theodore Roosevelt*, (New York: Billington and Sons, 1937), p. 277.
120. Maurice Fulton, ed., *Roosevelt's Writings*, (New York: Macmillan, 1922), pp. xx-xxi.
121. Maurice Fulton, ed., *Roosevelt's Writings*, (New York: Macmillan, 1922), pp. xx-xxi.
122. Maurice Fulton, ed., *Roosevelt's Writings*, (New York: Macmillan, 1922), p. xix.
123. Clarence Carson, *The Growth of America*, (Greenville, AL: American Textbook Committee, 1981), p. 235.
124. James Dallimore, *The Long Shadow*, (New York: Allan and Digby, 1962), p. 284.
125. Hebrews 11:4, KJV.
126. Thomas Russell, ed., *Life and Work of Theodore Roosevelt*, (New York: L.H. Walter), p. 257.
127. Edward Wagenknecht, *The Seven Worlds of Theodore Roosevelt*, (New York: Longmans and Green, 1958), p. 165.
128. Theodore Roosevelt, *The Foes of Our Own Household*, (New York: Charles Scribner's Sons, 1926), p. 149.
129. Maurice Fulton, ed., *Roosevelt's Writings*, (New York: Macmillan, 1922), p. 29.
130. Thomas Russell, ed., *Life and Work of Theodore Roosevelt*, (New York: L.H. Walter, 1919), p. 288.
131. Thomas Russell, ed., *Life and Work of Theodore Roosevelt*, (New York: L.H. Walter, 1919), p. 289.
132. Thomas Russell, ed., *Life and Work of Theodore Roosevelt*, (New York: L.H. Walter, 1919), p. 289.
133. Theodore Roosevelt, *Realizable Ideals*, (New York: Scribners, 1925), p. 665.
134. Theodore Roosevelt, *Autobiography*, (New York: Scribners, 1924), p. vii.
135. Theodore Roosevelt, *Autobiography*, (New York: Scribners, 1924), p. 7.
136. Jacob Riis, *Theodore Roosevelt the Citizen*, (New York: Macmillan, 1904), p. 444.
137. Jacob Riis, *Theodore Roosevelt the Citizen*, (New York: Macmillan, 1904), p. 445.
138. Theodore Roosevelt, *Autobiography*, (New York: Scribners, 1924), p. 8.
139. Theodore Roosevelt, *Autobiography*, (New York: Scribners, 1924), p. 8.
140. Jacob Riis, *Theodore Roosevelt the Citizen*, (New York: Macmillan, 1904), p. 447.
141. Jacob Riis, *Theodore Roosevelt the Citizen*, (New York: Macmillan, 1904), p. 445.
142. Jacob Riis, *Theodore Roosevelt the Citizen*, (New York: Macmillan, 1904), p. 445.

143. James Austin Wills, *The Letters and Speeches of Theodore Roosevelt*, (New York: Billington and Sons, 1937), p. 76.
144. Horace Goldman, *The Strenuous Life*, (New York: George Dial, 1958), p. 38.
145. Horace Goldman, *The Strenuous Life*, (New York: George Dial, 1958), p. 39.
146. Horace Goldman, *The Strenuous Life*, (New York: George Dial, 1958), p. 39.
147. Maurice Fulton, ed., *Roosevelt's Writings*, (New York: Macmillan, 1922), p. 166.
148. Horace Goldman, *The Strenuous Life*, (New York: George Dial, 1958), p. 39.
149. Maurice Fulton, ed., *Roosevelt's Writings*, (New York: Macmillan, 1922), p. 68.
150. Maurice Fulton, ed., *Roosevelt's Writings*, (New York: Macmillan, 1922), p. xiv.
151. Thomas Russell, ed., *Life and Work of Theodore Roosevelt*, (New York: L.H. Walter), p. 312.
152. Thomas Russell, ed., *Life and Work of Theodore Roosevelt*, (New York: L.H. Walter), p. 312.
153. Thomas Russell, ed., *Life and Work of Theodore Roosevelt*, (New York: L.H. Walter), p. 209.
154. Edward Wagenknecht, *The Seven Worlds of Theodore Roosevelt*, (New York: Longmans and Green, 1958), p.38.
155. Edward Wagenknecht, *The Seven Worlds of Theodore Roosevelt*, (New York: Longmans and Green, 1958), p. 45.
156. Lyman Abbot, ed., *A Guide to Reading*, (New York: Doubleday, 1917), p. 120.
157. Edward Wagenknecht, *The Seven Worlds of Theodore Roosevelt*, (New York: Longmans and Green, 1958), p. 76.
158. Edward Wagenknecht, *The Seven Worlds of Theodore Roosevelt*, (New York: Longmans and Green, 1958) p. 44.
159. Edward Wagenknecht, *The Seven Worlds of Theodore Roosevelt*, (New York: Longmans and Green, 1958), p. 44.
160. Edward Wagenknecht, *The Seven Worlds of Theodore Roosevelt*, (New York: Longmans and Green, 1958), p. 33.
161. Edward Wagenknecht, *The Seven Worlds of Theodore Roosevelt*, (New York: Longmans and Green, 1958) p. 32.
162. Edward Wagenknecht, *The Seven Worlds of Theodore Roosevelt*, (New York: Longmans and Green, 1958), p. 32.
163. Edward Wagenknecht, *The Seven Worlds of Theodore Roosevelt*, (New York: Longmans and Green, 1958) p. 32.
164. James Lever, *The Roosevelt Mythos*, (New York: Dorrit-Justin, 1923), p. 204.
165. David Johnson, *Theodore Roosevelt: American Monarch*, (Philadelphia: American History Sources, 1981), p. 73.
166. Edward Wagenknecht, *The Seven Worlds of Theodore Roosevelt*, (New York: Longmans and Green, 1958), p. 8.
167. Edward Wagenknecht, *The Seven Worlds of Theodore Roosevelt*, (New York: Longmans and Green, 1958), p. 6.
168. James Lever, *The Roosevelt Mythos*, (New York: Dorrit-Justin, 1923), p. 191.
169. James Lever, *The Roosevelt Mythos*, (New York: Dorrit-Justin, 1923), p. 191.
170. James Lever, *The Roosevelt Mythos*, (New York: Dorrit-Justin, 1923), p. 192.
171. James Lever, *The Roosevelt Mythos*, (New York: Dorrit-Justin, 1923), p. 192.
172. James Austin Wills, *The Letters and Speeches of Theodore Roosevelt*, (New York: Billington and Sons, 1937), p. 94.
173. Proverbs 29:18, KJV.
174. Edward Wagenknecht, *The Seven Worlds of Theodore Roosevelt*, (New York: Longmans and Green, 1958), p. 1.
175. Richard III, I:151.
176. Edward Wagenknecht, *The Seven Worlds of Theodore Roosevelt*, (New York: Longmans and Green, 1958), p. 181.
177. Edward Wagenknecht, *The Seven Worlds of Theodore Roosevelt*, (New York: Longmans and Green, 1958), p. 181.
178. Maurice Fulton, ed., *Roosevelt's Writings*, (New York: Macmillan, 1922), p. xxvi.
179. Rod Evans and Irwin Berent, eds., *The Quotable Conservative*, (Holbrook, MA: Adams, 1995), p. 40.
180. Theodore Roosevelt, *The Foes of Our Own Household*, (New York: Charles Scribner's Sons, 1926), p. 47.
181. Theodore Roosevelt, *The Foes of Our Own Household*, (New York: Charles Scribner's Sons, 1926), p. 47.
182. Maurice Fulton, ed., *Roosevelt's Writings*, (New York: Macmillan, 1922), p. 155.
183. Maurice Fulton, ed., *Roosevelt's Writings*, (New York: Macmillan, 1922), p. 36.
184. James Lever, *The Roosevelt Mythos*, (New York: Dorrit-Justin, 1923), p. 59.
185. Archibald Roosevelt, ed., *Race, Riots, Reds, and Crime*, (New York: Roosevelt Memorial Association, 1939), p. 101.

186. James Austin Wills, *The Letters and Speeches of Theodore Roosevelt*, (New York: Billington and Sons, 1937), p. 81.

187. Jonathan Hewlitt, *The American Impact*, (London: Caprice and Meadows, 1956), p. 21.

188. James Austin Wills, *The Letters and Speeches of Theodore Roosevelt*, (New York: Billington and Sons, 1937), p. 56.

189. James Austin Wills, *The Letters and Speeches of Theodore Roosevelt*, (New York: Billington and Sons, 1937), p. 58.

190. James Austin Wills, *The Letters and Speeches of Theodore Roosevelt*, (New York: Billington and Sons, 1937), p. 58.

191. James Austin Wills, *The Letters and Speeches of Theodore Roosevelt*, (New York: Billington and Sons, 1937), p. 58.

192. James Austin Wills, *The Letters and Speeches of Theodore Roosevelt*, (New York: Billington and Sons, 1937), p. xli.

193. James Austin Wills, *The Letters and Speeches of Theodore Roosevelt*, (New York: Billington and Sons, 1937), p. xli.

194. Maurice Fulton, ed., *Roosevelt's Writings*, (New York: Macmillan, 1922), p. 200.

195. James Austin Wills, *The Letters and Speeches of Theodore Roosevelt*, (New York: Billington and Sons, 1937), p. 46.

196. James Austin Wills, *The Letters and Speeches of Theodore Roosevelt*, (New York: Billington and Sons, 1937), p. 2.

197. James Austin Wills, *The Letters and Speeches of Theodore Roosevelt*, (New York: Billington and Sons, 1937), p. 451.

198. Theodore Roosevelt, *Presidential Addresses and Papers*, vol. I, (New York: Review of Reviews, 1910), p. 231.

199. James Austin Wills, *The Letters and Speeches of Theodore Roosevelt*, (New York: Billington and Sons, 1937), p. 232.

200. James Lever, *The Roosevelt Mythos*, (New York: Dorrit-Justin, 1923), p. 206.

201. Jonathan Hewlitt, *The American Impact*, (London: Caprice and Meadows, 1956), p. 202.

202. Henry Cabot Lodge and Theodore Roosevelt, *Hero Tales from American History*, (New York: Century, 1895), p. xxiii.

203. G. K. Chesterton, *Omnibus*, (London: Stratford Lewes, 1966), pp. 142-143.

204. Jonathan Hewlitt, *The American Impact*, (London: Caprice and Meadows, 1956), p. 202.

205. Jonathan Hewlitt, *The American Impact*, (London: Caprice and Meadows, 1956), p. 203.

206. Edward Wagenknecht, *The Seven Worlds of Theodore Roosevelt*, (New York: Longmans and Green, 1958), p. 151.

207. Edward Wagenknecht, *The Seven Worlds of Theodore Roosevelt*, (New York: Longmans and Green, 1958), p. 152.

208. James Austin Wills, *The Letters and Speeches of Theodore Roosevelt*, (New York: Billington and Sons, 1937), p. 288.

209. Edward Wagenknecht, *The Seven Worlds of Theodore Roosevelt*, (New York: Longmans and Green, 1958), p. 155.

210. Edward Wagenknecht, *The Seven Worlds of Theodore Roosevelt*, (New York: Longmans and Green, 1958), p. 152.

211. Maurice Fulton, ed., *Roosevelt's Writings*, (New York: Macmillan, 1922), p. 79.

212. Maurice Fulton, ed., *Roosevelt's Writings*, (New York: Macmillan, 1922), p. 79.

213. James Austin Wills, *The Letters and Speeches of Theodore Roosevelt*, (New York: Billington and Sons, 1937), p. 202.

214. James Austin Wills, *The Letters and Speeches of Theodore Roosevelt*, (New York: Billington and Sons, 1937), p. 88.

215. James Austin Wills, *The Letters and Speeches of Theodore Roosevelt*, (New York: Billington and Sons, 1937), p. 202.

216. James Austin Wills, *The Letters and Speeches of Theodore Roosevelt*, (New York: Billington and Sons, 1937), p. 202.

217. James Austin Wills, *The Letters and Speeches of Theodore Roosevelt*, (New York: Billington and Sons, 1937), p. 202.

218. David Johnson, *Theodore Roosevelt: American Monarch*, (Philadelphia: American History Sources, 1981), p. 288.

219. Mark Hammond Lowe, *Roosevelt and War*, (New York: Garamond, 1922), p. 15.

220. Thomas Russell, ed., *Life and Work of Theodore Roosevelt*, (New York: L. H. Walter, 1919), p. 205.

221. Mark Hammond Lowe, *Roosevelt and War*, (New York: Garamond, 1922), p. 17.

222. Edward Wagenknecht, *The Seven Worlds of Theodore Roosevelt*, (New York: Longmans and Green, 1958), p. 38.
223. Edward Wagenknecht, *The Seven Worlds of Theodore Roosevelt*, (New York: Longmans and Green, 1958), p. 42.
224. James Lever, *The Roosevelt Mythos*, (New York: Dorrit-Justin, 1923), p. 43.
225. Edward Wagenknecht, *The Seven Worlds of Theodore Roosevelt*, (New York: Longmans and Green, 1958), p. 42.
226. David Johnson, *Theodore Roosevelt: American Monarch*, (Philadelphia: American History Sources, 1981), p. 44.
227. David Johnson, *Theodore Roosevelt: American Monarch*, (Philadelphia: American History Sources, 1981), p. 44.
228. Nathan Miller, *Theodore Roosevelt: A Life*, (New York: William Morrow, 1992), p. 511.
229. James Lever, *The Roosevelt Mythos*, (New York: Dorrit-Justin, 1923), p. 48.
230. Nathan Miller, *Theodore Roosevelt: A Life*, (New York: William Morrow, 1992), p. 37.
231. Thomas Russell, ed., *Life and Work of Theodore Roosevelt*, (New York: L. H. Walter, 1919), p. 85.
232. Edward Wagenknecht, *The Seven Worlds of Theodore Roosevelt*, (New York: Longmans and Green, 1958), p. 80.
233. Maurice Fulton, ed., *Roosevelt's Writings*, (New York: Macmillan, 1922), p. xviii.
234. Maurice Fulton, ed., *Roosevelt's Writings*, (New York: Macmillan, 1922), p. xix.
235. James Lever, *The Roosevelt Mythos*, (New York: Dorrit-Justin, 1923), p. 46.
236. Thomas Russell, ed., *Life and Work of Theodore Roosevelt*, (New York: L. H. Walter, 1919, p. 361.
237. James Lever, *The Roosevelt Mythos*, (New York: Dorrit-Justin, 1923), p. 46.
238. James Lever, *The Roosevelt Mythos*, (New York: Dorrit-Justin, 1923), p. 48.
239. James Austin Wills, *The Letters and Speeches of Theodore Roosevelt*, (New York: Billington and Sons, 1937), p. 111.
240. Edward Wagenknecht, *The Seven Worlds of Theodore Roosevelt*, (New York: Longmans and Green, 1958), p. 16.
241. Maurice Fulton, ed., *Roosevelt's Writings*, (New York: Macmillan, 1922), p. 29.
242. James Lever, *The Roosevelt Mythos*, (New York: Dorrit-Justin, 1923), p. vii.
243. James Lever, *The Roosevelt Mythos*, (New York: Dorrit-Justin, 1923), p. viii.
244. Maurice Fulton, ed., *Roosevelt's Writings*, (New York: Macmillan, 1922), p. 168.
245. James Lever, *The Roosevelt Mythos*, (New York: Dorrit-Justin, 1923), p. 88.
246. James Lever, *The Roosevelt Mythos*, (New York: Dorrit-Justin, 1923), p. 88.
247. Edward Wagenknecht, *The Seven Worlds of Theodore Roosevelt*, (New York: Longmans and Green, 1958), p. 162.
248. Edward Wagenknecht, *The Seven Worlds of Theodore Roosevelt*, (New York: Longmans and Green, 1958), p. 162.
249. Edward Wagenknecht, *The Seven Worlds of Theodore Roosevelt*, (New York: Longmans and Green, 1958), p. 162.
250. James Lever, *The Roosevelt Mythos*, (New York: Dorrit-Justin, 1923), p. 89.
251. David Johnson, *Theodore Roosevelt: American Monarch*, (Philadelphia: American History Sources, 1981), p. 322.
252. David Johnson, *Theodore Roosevelt: American Monarch*, (Philadelphia: American History Sources, 1981), p. 323.
253. Edward Wagenknecht, *The Seven Worlds of Theodore Roosevelt*, (New York: Longmans and Green, 1958), p. 114.
254. Edward Wagenknecht, *The Seven Worlds of Theodore Roosevelt*, (New York: Longmans and Green, 1958), p. 110.
255. Edward Wagenknecht, *The Seven Worlds of Theodore Roosevelt*, (New York: Longmans and Green, 1958), p. 8.
256. James Lever, *The Roosevelt Mythos*, (New York: Dorrit-Justin, 1923), p. 44.
257. Edward Wagenknecht, *The Seven Worlds of Theodore Roosevelt*, (New York: Longmans and Green, 1958), p. 111.
258. Edward Wagenknecht, *The Seven Worlds of Theodore Roosevelt*, (New York: Longmans and Green, 1958), p. 111.
259. Edward Wagenknecht, *The Seven Worlds of Theodore Roosevelt*, (New York: Longmans and Green, 1958), p. 111.
260. James Lever, *The Roosevelt Mythos*, (New York: Dorrit-Justin, 1923), p. xiv.
261. James Lever, *The Roosevelt Mythos*, (New York: Dorrit-Justin, 1923), p. xiv.
262. Edward Wagenknecht, *The Seven Worlds of Theodore Roosevelt*, (New York: Longmans and Green, 1958), p. 111.

263. James Lever, *The Roosevelt Mythos*, (New York: Dorrit-Justin, 1923), p. 191.
264. Theodore Roosevelt, *The Foes of Our Own Household*, (New York: George H. Doran, 1917), p. 168.
265. David Johnson, *Theodore Roosevelt: American Monarch*, (Philadelphia: American History Sources, 1981), p. 44.
266. David Johnson, *Theodore Roosevelt: American Monarch*, (Philadelphia: American History Sources, 1981), p. 44.
267. David Johnson, *Theodore Roosevelt: American Monarch*, (Philadelphia: American History Sources, 1981), p. 44.
268. Theodore Roosevelt, *The Foes of Our Own Household*, (New York: George H. Doran, 1917), p. 152.
269. David Kennedy, *Birth Control in America: The Career of Margaret Sanger*, (New Haven, CT: Yale University Press), pp. 146-147.
270. David Kennedy, *Birth Control in America: The Career of Margaret Sanger*, (New Haven, CT: Yale University Press), pp. 146-147.
271. Edward Wagenknecht, *The Seven Worlds of Theodore Roosevelt*, (New York: Longmans and Green, 1958), p. 86.
272. Theodore Roosevelt, *The Foes of Our Own Household*, (New York: George H. Doran, 1917), p. 152.
273. Theodore Roosevelt, *The Foes of Our Own Household*, (New York: George H. Doran, 1917), p. 152.
274. The Woman Rebel, June 1914.
275. The Woman Rebel, June 1914.
276. James Austin Wills, *The Letters and Speeches of Theodore Roosevelt*, (New York: Billington and Sons, 1937), p. 56.
277. Theodore Roosevelt, *Social Justice and Popular Rule*, (New York: Scribner's, 1926), p. 334.
278. Theodore Roosevelt, *Social Justice and Popular Rule*, (New York: Scribner's, 1926), p. 335.
279. James Austin Wills, *The Letters and Speeches of Theodore Roosevelt*, (New York: Billington and Sons, 1937), p. 234.
280. James Austin Wills, *The Letters and Speeches of Theodore Roosevelt*, (New York: Billington and Sons, 1937), p. 23.
281. Thomas Dyer, *Theodore Roosevelt and the Idea of Race*, (Baton Rouge, LA: Louisiana State University, 1980), p. 105.
282. Maurice Fulton, ed., *Roosevelt's Writings*, (New York: Macmillan, 1922), p. 165.
283. Edward Wagenknecht, *The Seven Worlds of Theodore Roosevelt*, (New York: Longmans and Green, 1958), p. 186.
284. Edward Wagenknecht, *The Seven Worlds of Theodore Roosevelt*, (New York: Longmans and Green, 1958), p. 186.
285. Thomas Dyer, *Theodore Roosevelt and the Idea of Race*, (Baton Rouge, LA: Louisiana State University, 1980), p. 105.
286. David Johnson, *Theodore Roosevelt: American Monarch*, (Philadelphia: American History Sources, 1981, p. 356.
287. David Johnson, *Theodore Roosevelt: American Monarch*, (Philadelphia: American History Sources, 1981, p. 356.
288. David Johnson, *Theodore Roosevelt: American Monarch*, (Philadelphia: American History Sources, 1981, p. 356.
289. Thomas Russell, ed., *Life and Work of Theodore Roosevelt*, (New York: L.H. Walter, 1919), p. 261.
290. David Johnson, *Theodore Roosevelt: American Monarch*, (Philadelphia: American History Sources, 1981), p. 1.
291. Maurice Fulton, ed., *Roosevelt's Writings*, (New York: Macmillan, 1922), p. 16.
292. David Johnson, *Theodore Roosevelt: American Monarch*, (Philadelphia: American History Sources, 1981), p. 109.
293. Theodore Roosevelt and Henry Cabot Lodge, *Hero Tales from American History*, (New York: Scribner's, 1926), p. xxiii.
294. Theodore Roosevelt and Henry Cabot Lodge, *Hero Tales from American History*, (New York: Scribner's, 1926), p. xxiii.
295. Maurice Fulton, ed., *Roosevelt's Writings*, (New York: Macmillan, 1922), p. x.
296. Maurice Fulton, ed., *Roosevelt's Writings*, (New York: Macmillan, 1922), p. xxxiv.
297. Maurice Fulton, ed., *Roosevelt's Writings*, (New York: Macmillan, 1922), p. xxxiv.
298. Lord Charnwood, *Theodore Roosevelt*, (Boston: Atlantic Monthly, 1923), p. 47.
299. Thomas Russell, ed., *Life and Work of Theodore Roosevelt*, (New York: L.H. Walter), p. 122.
300. Thomas Russell, ed., *Life and Work of Theodore Roosevelt*, (New York: L.H. Walter), p. 123.
301. David Johnson, *Theodore Roosevelt: American Monarch*, (Philadelphia: American History Sources, 1981), p. 274.
302. Maurice Fulton, ed., *Roosevelt's Writings*, (New York: Macmillan, 1922), p. xxxiv.

303. David Johnson, *Theodore Roosevelt: American Monarch*, (Philadelphia: American History Sources, 1981), p. 276.

304. Theodore Roosevelt, *The Foes of Our Own Household*, (New York: George H. Doran, 1917), p. 130.

305. Edward Wagenknecht, *The Seven Worlds of Theodore Roosevelt*, (New York: Longmans and Green, 1958), p. 182.

306. Mark Hammond Lowe, *Roosevelt and War*, (New York: Garamond, 1922), p. 49.

307. Theodore Roosevelt, *The Foes of Our Own Household*, (New York: George H. Doran, 1917), p. 132.

308. Theodore Roosevelt, *Autobiography*, (New York: Scribners, 1924), p. 11.

309. *Trinity Hymnal*, (Atlanta, GA: Great Commission, 1990), p. 94.

310. Edward Wagenknecht, *The Seven Worlds of Theodore Roosevelt*, (New York: Longmans and Green, 1958), p. 182.

311. Robert Crunden, *Ministers of Reform: The Progressives' Achievement in American Civilization, 1889-1920*, (New York: Basic Books, 1982), p. 3.

312. James Austin Wills, *The Letters and Speeches of Theodore Roosevelt*, (New York: Billington and Sons, 1937), p. 86.

313. James Austin Wills, *The Letters and Speeches of Theodore Roosevelt*, (New York: Billington and Sons, 1937), p. 90.

314. James Lever, *The Roosevelt Mythos*, (New York: Dorrit-Justin, 1923), p. 191.

315. Jonathan Hewlitt, *The American Impact*, (London: Caprice and Meadows, 1956), p. 174.

316. James Austin Wills, *The Letters and Speeches of Theodore Roosevelt*, (New York: Billington and Sons, 1937), p. 59.

317. James Lever, *The Roosevelt Mythos*, (New York: Dorrit-Justin, 1923), 191.

318. James Lever, *The Roosevelt Mythos*, (New York: Dorrit-Justin, 1923), 192.

319. James Austin Wills, *The Letters and Speeches of Theodore Roosevelt*, (New York: Billington and Sons, 1937), p. 254.

320. David Johnson, *Theodore Roosevelt: American Monarch*, (Philadelphia: American History Sources, 1981), p. 91.

321. Edward Wagenknecht, *The Seven Worlds of Theodore Roosevelt*, (New York: Longmans and Green, 1958), p. 183.

322. David Johnson, *Theodore Roosevelt: American Monarch*, (Philadelphia: American History Sources, 1981), p. 33.

323. David Johnson, *Theodore Roosevelt: American Monarch*, (Philadelphia: American History Sources, 1981), p. 98.

324. Theodore Roosevelt, *Foes of Our Own Household*, (New York: Scribners, 1926), p. 3.

325. George Grant, *The Blood of the Moon: The Roots of the Middle East Crisis*, (Brentwood, TN: Wolgemuth & Hyatt, 1991), pp. 105-107.

326. David Johnson, *Theodore Roosevelt: American Monarch*, (Philadelphia: American History Sources, 1981), p. 229.

327. David Johnson, *Theodore Roosevelt: American Monarch*, (Philadelphia: American History Sources, 1981), p. 229.

328. Thomas Russell, ed., *Life and Work of Theodore Roosevelt*, (New York: L. H. Walter, 1919), p. 261.

329. David Johnson, *Theodore Roosevelt: American Monarch*, (Philadelphia: American History Sources, 1981), p. 229.

330. Robert Crunden, *Ministers of Reform: The Progressives' Achievement in American Civilization, 1889-1920*, (New York: Basic Books, 1982), p. 3.

331. Maurice Fulton, ed., *Roosevelt's Writings*, (New York: Macmillan, 1922), p. 73.

332. Jonathan Hewlitt, *The American Impact*, (London: Caprice and Meadows, 1956), p. vi.

333. Thomas Russell, ed., *Life and Work of Theodore Roosevelt*, (New York: L. H. Walter, 1919), p. 262.

334. James Lever, *The Roosevelt Mythos*, (New York: Dorrit-Justin, 1923), p. 322.

335. Nathan Miller, *Theodore Roosevelt: A Life*, (New York: William Morrow, 1992), p. 566.

336. Thomas Russell, ed., *Life and Work of Theodore Roosevelt*, (New York: L.H. Walter, 1919), p. 276.

337. Maurice Fulton, ed., *Roosevelt's Writings*, (New York: Macmillan, 1922), p. 166.

338. Edward Wagenknecht, *The Seven Worlds of Theodore Roosevelt*, (New York: Longmans and Green, 1958), p. 3.

339. James Lever, *The Roosevelt Mythos*, (New York: Dorrit-Justin, 1923), p. 2.

340. Colossians 4:5, ASV.

341. Edward Wagenknecht, *The Seven Worlds of Theodore Roosevelt*, (New York: Longmans and Green, 1958), p. 4.

342. James Lever, *The Roosevelt Mythos*, (New York: Dorrit-Justin, 1923), p. 2.

343. James Austin Wills, *The Letters and Speeches of Theodore Roosevelt*, (New York: Billington and Sons, 1937), p. 36.

344. James Austin Wills, *The Letters and Speeches of Theodore Roosevelt*, (New York: Billington and Sons, 1937), p. 36.

345. Theodore Roosevelt, *Foes of Our Own Household*, (New York: Scribners, 1926), p. 3.

346. Theodore Roosevelt, *Foes of Our Own Household*, (New York: Scribners, 1926), p. 152.

347. Theodore Roosevelt, *Foes of Our Own Household*, (New York: Scribners, 1926), p. 132.

348. Theodore Roosevelt, *Foes of Our Own Household*, (New York: Scribners, 1926), p. 132.

349. Theodore Roosevelt, *Foes of Our Own Household*, (New York: Scribners, 1926), p. 132.

350. Theodore Roosevelt, *Foes of Our Own Household*, (New York: Scribners, 1926), pp. 132-133.

351. James Austin Wills, *The Letters and Speeches of Theodore Roosevelt*, (New York: Billington and Sons, 1937), p. 59.

352. James Austin Wills, *The Letters and Speeches of Theodore Roosevelt*, (New York: Billington and Sons, 1937), p. 60.

353. James Austin Wills, *The Letters and Speeches of Theodore Roosevelt*, (New York: Billington and Sons, 1937), p. 60.

354. James Carter Braxton, *Gouverneur Morris*, (Charleston, SC: Braden-Lowell Press, 1911), p. 101.

355. James Carter Braxton, *Gouverneur Morris*, (Charleston, SC: Braden-Lowell Press, 1911), p. 101.

356. James Austin Wills, *The Letters and Speeches of Theodore Roosevelt*, (New York: Billington and Sons, 1937), p. 34.

357. Theodore Roosevelt, *Realizable Ideals*, (New York: Scribners, 1924), p. 650.

358. James Austin Wills, *The Letters and Speeches of Theodore Roosevelt*, (New York: Billington and Sons, 1937), p. 34.

359. James Austin Wills, *The Letters and Speeches of Theodore Roosevelt*, (New York: Billington and Sons, 1937), p. 67.

360. James Austin Wills, *The Letters and Speeches of Theodore Roosevelt*, (New York: Billington and Sons, 1937), p. 67.

361. James Austin Wills, *The Letters and Speeches of Theodore Roosevelt*, (New York: Billington and Sons, 1937), p. 68.

362. Fernanda Eberstadt, *Isaac and His Devils*, (New York: Viking, 1990), p. 89.

363. George Washington, *Programs and Papers*, (Washington, DC: Washington Bicentennial Committee, 1932), p. 33.

364. E. A. Van Valkenburg, *The Inspiration of Theodore Roosevelt*, (New York: Scribners, 1924), p. 233.

365. E. A. Van Valkenburg, *The Inspiration of Theodore Roosevelt*, (New York: Scribners, 1924), pp. 233-234.

366. E. A. Van Valkenburg, *The Inspiration of Theodore Roosevelt*, (New York: Scribners, 1924), p. 234.

367. Horace Goldman, *The Strenuous Life*, (New York: George Dial, 1958), p. 39.

368. Edward Wagenknecht, *The Seven Worlds of Theodore Roosevelt*, (New York: Longmans and Green, 1958), p. 44.